Prospecting 4.0
A Modern Way to
Ancient Battles

FC Bohnke

Copyright © 2021
All rights reserved.

No part of this book may be reproduced by any means whatsoever without the written permission of the author, except for very brief portions of the book which may be quoted for the purpose of review.

TABLE OF CONTENTS

INTRODUCTION 4

CHAPTER 1: THE AIMS OF B2B PROSPECTING 8

CHAPTER 2: HOW TO IDENTIFY THE IDEAL B2B CUSTOMER 23

CHAPTER 3: STAY CONNECTED TO NON-SALES READY LEADS 38

CHAPTER 4: HOW TO INCREASE LANDING PAGE CONVERSION RATES 53

CHAPTER 5: MAKE THE BEST OF WHAT YOU'VE GOT 58

CHAPTER 6: WHAT EXACTLY IS B2B MARKETING? 83

CHAPTER 7: HOW TO DEVELOP A SOLID B2B MARKETING STRATEGY 88

CHAPTER 8: MOVING FROM STRATEGY TO REALITY 107

INTRODUCTION

I can't tell you how many prospecting books I have read about prospecting in the business to consumer market. But what about prospecting for businesses? This is a topic that isn't discussed enough, so here's my take on it. First of all, prospecting in the business-to-business sector can be a daunting process with its own set of challenges and best practices that prospectors need to be aware of before prospecting. The prospector needs to do research on potential customers by using sources such as websites, blogs, publications, directories, social media networks, etc. and then call them up and talk about their product or service without sounding too pushy. It's not easy, but it is possible with the right techniques and best practices. Prospectors should prospect as long as they feel necessary because prospecting is an ongoing marketing strategy. Prospecting techniques that work best include finding target companies with a business model suited for your offering; keeping track of new businesses entering an industry so you know who they are targeting, setting up Google alerts if you prospect using newsletters or trade publications, etc. Prospects can be found all throughout social media and online resources like Twitter, LinkedIn and company websites. The prospector searches for potential leads by using sources such as websites, blogs, publications, directories, social media networks etc. This book will cover prospecting techniques that work for prospectors who are looking into the B2B market.

But first, these are **7 important mindsets you need to have as a prospector in the B2B market in the XXI century.**

Highly successful people, from ancient philosophers like Aristotle to modern-day thought leaders, have always made the point that there is little need to "reinvent the wheel." If you study what successful people do, you find patterns. When you duplicate those patterns, you'll be able to duplicate their success.

Developing and maintaining a fanatical prospecting mindset is the ultimate key to success in sales. This mindset keeps you focused, persistent, and driven to open doors in the face of inevitable setbacks, challenges, and rejection. When you adopt a fanatical prospecting mindset, you'll grow in the face of adversity rather than shrink before it.

I've spent a lifetime studying fanatical prospectors. Along the way I discovered seven core mindsets that define them. These are their success clues. Duplicate these mindsets and you'll guarantee yourself success in filling your pipeline and crushing your number.

1. Optimistic and enthusiastic: Fanatical prospectors have a winning, optimistic mindset. They know that negative, bitter people with a victim mindset do not succeed in sales. Fanatical prospectors attack each day with enthusiasm; fired up and ready to rock. They view each day as a fresh new opportunity to achieve. Because of this, they seize the day, brush past naysayers and complainers, and dive into prospecting with unequaled drive. Even on bad days they reach deep inside and find enough stored enthusiasm to push themselves to keep going and make one more call.

2. Competitive: Fanatical prospectors view prospecting through the eyes of a fierce competitor. They are hardwired to win and will do whatever it takes to stay on

top. They begin each day prepared to win the battle for the attention of the most coveted prospects, and outwit and outhustle their competitors at every turn.

3. Confident: Fanatical prospectors approach prospecting with confidence. They expect to win and believe they are going to win. They have developed mental toughness and the ability to manage the disruptive emotions of fear, uncertainty, and doubt. They leverage confidence and self-control to persuade prospects to give up time and resources to engage in sales conversations.

4. Relentless: Fanatical prospectors have a high need for achievement. They do whatever it takes to reach their goal. They never, ever give up believing that persistence always wins. They use rejection as motivational fuel to get up and keep going with a determined belief that their next "yes" is right around the corner.

5. Thirsty for knowledge: Fanatical prospectors welcome feedback and coaching. They seek out every opportunity to learn and invest in themselves by voraciously consuming books, podcasts, audiobooks, blog posts, online training, live seminars, and anything else they believe will make them better. They have an unshakable belief that everything happens for a reason and through this lens view setbacks as opportunities to learn and grow.

6. Systematic and efficient: Fanatical prospectors have the ability to execute with near-robotic and systematical efficiency. They are skilled at their craft like a pro athlete. They protect the golden hours, block their time, and concentrate their power to tune out distractions and avoid disruptions. They systematically develop their prospect database to build more effective and targeted lists, and squeeze every moment from each sales day.

7. Adaptive and flexible: Fanatical prospectors have acute situational awareness. Because of this, they are able to respond and adapt quickly to changing situations and circumstances. They leverage the three As in their approach to prospecting: adopt, adapt, adept. They actively search out and adopt new ideas and best practices, then adapt them as their own, and work at it until they become adept at execution. Fanatical prospectors are constantly trying new things and flexing with the world around them—whatever it takes to keep their pipeline full. They tend to be early adopters of new prospecting techniques, cutting-edge technology, and game-changing tactics.

Look around you. I guarantee that you will find that the highest-earning sales professionals in your town, city, networking groups, and company are fanatical prospectors. From insurance to real estate to industrial products to software to mobile to autos to trucks to medical device and pharmaceutical—in every industry and every company—they share these seven mindsets.

As you move forward through this book, use these seven mindsets as a foundational reference point to assess where you have room to grow and further develop your mindset.

CHAPTER 1:

THE AIMS OF B2B PROSPECTING

"I don't focus on what I'm up against. I focus on my goals and I try to ignore the rest.",Venus Williams .

"If you don't know where you're going, you might end up someplace else." The great and oft-quoted Yogi Berra said those words. Sadly, this is how many salespeople approach prospecting,on a wing and a prayer.

From the get-go I've been clear that my objective is to teach you how to be both efficient and effective with prospecting. Another way to say this is balancing quantity with quality.

Knowing your objective for each call makes you more efficient because you are able to build prospecting blocks and group your prospecting channel touches around those objectives. This allows you to move faster and make more prospecting touches in less time. We'll discu, "Leveraging the Prospecting Pyramid."

Developing a defined objective makes you effective because on each prospecting call, e-mail, social media touch, networking event, or referral request, you know exactly what to ask for and how to bridge to your prospect's problems to give them a compelling reason to accept your request.

The objective is the primary outcome you expect from your prospecting touch. There are four core prospective objectives:

1. Set an appointment.

2. Gather information and qualify.

3. Close a sale.

4. Build familiarity.

Your situation, industry, prospect base, product, and service are unique, as will be your prospecting objectives. Here are some quick rules of thumb to get you started when developing prospecting objectives:

1. If you are selling a complex, high-risk, high-cost product or service, your primary objective will most often be an appointment with a qualified decision maker, influencer, or other stakeholder who can help you move the deal forward. Your secondary objective will be to gather information. Your tertiary objective will be to build familiarity.

2. If you are selling a transactional, low-risk, low-cost product or service and you are in inside sales, your primary objective will be closing the sale and secondarily gathering information.

3. If you are selling a transactional, low-risk, low-cost product and you are in outside sales and prospecting via any channel other than in person (phone, e-mail, text, social), your primary objective will be to set an appointment and secondarily to gather information. If you are prospecting in person ("knocking" on the prospect's door), your primary objective will be to close the deal.

4. If you have a highly qualified database of prospects in your CRM, the primary objective of most of your prospecting calls will be setting appointments as the buying window opens to start the sales process. The secondary objective will be building familiarity to increase the probability that your prospect will engage when the buying window opens.

5. If the product or service you are selling can only be purchased during specific buying windows, like when a contract expires or within a defined budgetary period, gathering information to qualify the buying window will be your primary objective and building familiarity your secondary objective with most calls. You don't want to waste setting an appointment with a prospect that cannot buy because of contractual or budgetary handcuffs. Once you have identified the buying window, your primary objective will shift to setting an appointment.

6. If you are new in your territory or working for a start-up or new division, your primary objective will be gathering information so you can identify decision makers and qualify buying windows and budgets. The secondary objective will be to build familiarity.

Lots of salespeople stumble from unqualified prospect to unqualified prospect and wonder why, at the end of the day, week, or month, they sold nothing. This is why it is so important to have an objective for every prospecting touch.

Prospecting Is a Contact Sport

Prospecting, in many ways, is a brutal contact sport that shuns the nuance, art, and finesse of moving a deal through the sales pipe. To be effective, you've got to know what you want and ask for it. To be efficient, you've got to get in as many prospecting touches as possible during each prospecting block.

Prospecting is not for building relationships, selling, or chatting up your buyer. It is for setting the appointment, qualifying, building familiarity, and when it makes sense, moving into the sales process right on the spot. You don't need brilliant scripts. You don't need complex strategies. You don't need to overcomplicate it.

You have no time to waste on small talk, chitchat, or long-winded scripts (or e-mails) written by some dude in marketing who has never been within 50 feet of a prospect. You've got to get to the point, ask for what you want, and move on to the next touch.

Set an Appointment.

The most valuable activity in the sales process is a set appointment, no matter where you are in the pipe: initial meeting, discovery meetings, presentations, closing meetings, and so on.

To be absolutely clear, an appointment is a meeting that is on your calendar and your prospect's calendar; in other words, they are expecting you to show up in person or by phone, video call, or web conference at a specific time and date.

Many salespeople confuse "Just stop by," "I'll be here anytime," and "Call me maybe" statements from their prospects to be a commitment for an appointment. Let's not mince words. "Call me maybe" and "Just stop by anytime" are not appointments. To believe that they are, and to put them on your calendar as such, is pure delusion, and, as we've already learned, in sales you cannot be delusional and successful at the same time.

It is only an appointment when you have a firm commitment for a specific meeting time. Consider how much time is wasted driving to or calling into prospects who are not there because they never had a commitment to be there in the first place. Consider the emotional cost of believing you have firm commitments only to discover that you don't.

Working with prospects who are not committed to moving to the next step—either an initial meeting or a subsequent meeting—is like pushing a rope. You expend a tremendous amount of energy and emotion trying to move the deal forward, but you never get anywhere.

Recently I was working with an outbound inside rep who sells capital equipment to midmarket buyers in the manufacturing space. I followed up with him a few weeks after he and his peers attended a training program we designed for his company. Our dialog:

Me: "Armando, tell me how things are going."

Armando: (Sighs) "I guess okay?"

Me: "Okay? How do you mean?"

Armando: "Well, this appointment thing is not working for me."

Me: "How come?"

Armando: "I can't get anyone to show up."

Me: "What percentage of your appointments are no-shows?"

Armando: "I don't know, I guess around 80 percent of them."

Me: "Okay, tell me about the last one that was a no-show."

Armando: "I had a meeting schedule with Jessica Thomson, a buyer at Gogett International. She's never purchased anything from us before, and we had an appointment scheduled to review our line. When I called this morning at 10:00 AM she didn't answer the phone. I tried several more times until I got her assistant, who said she was traveling."

Me: "Did she accept the meeting request you sent via e-mail?"

Armando: "Well, um, I uh, didn't send one."

Me: "How come?"

Armando: "When I called her last week, she said she was super busy and would be happy to meet with me another time. She said she was usually available in the mornings and I could call anytime. I suggested 10:00 AM today and she said that would be fine, to just call her anytime."

Me: "Was that a real commitment to 10 AM on her part or more of a brush-off just to get you off of the phone?"

Armando: "I guess when you look at it that way, it was a brush-off."

Armando and I went through all the appointments he had on his calendar for the next seven days and not surprisingly, almost all of them were "call me maybe" noncommittal wishes he had accepted as real.

Delusion gets you nowhere. So here is a simple rule: It is only an appointment when it is on your calendar and your prospect's calendar and your prospect is expecting you to show up at a specific time, date, and place (physical or virtual).

Gather Information and Qualify

A good friend of mine is a big fan of a certain baseball League. It is a rite of passage that helps kids build character, hone their values, and learn how to win and lose.

Several years back, when his son played in the League, they were fortunate to be on a team with great coaches who invested their time to help their sons learn to love the game. Along the way, they helped their tight-knit group of parents learn a few lessons, too.

In one of their most intense games, they were in the bottom of the sixth inning with two outs and the bases loaded. The game was tied. With the winning run on third base, all they needed was a hit to win the game and advance to the play-offs.

As their next batter walked from the dugout toward the batter's box, the coach pulled him aside for one last pep talk. He kneeled in front of the 10-year-old young man, got a handful of his jersey near the collar, and gave him some sage advice.

"Whatever you do," the coach admonished, "don't swing at nothin' ugly."

As the Coach walked back to his position on the third base line, it struck him on how profound his coaching was when applied to sales and frankly, life.

If you've ever played baseball or softball or watched your kids play, you've no doubt witnessed a player chasing a wild pitch—too high, too low, or way outside of the strike zone. The awkward swing of the bat, swishing through thin air, leaves the player off-balance and embarrassed. It is sometimes funny to watch, but mostly the fans, coaches, and players just echo a collective groan and wonder why in the world the player took a swing at that pitch.

It is no different is sales. Each day salespeople waste time, energy, and emotion swinging at ugly deals. Deals that are unprofitable, unqualified, not in the buying window, don't have a budget, don't have an identified decision maker, or because of contracts don't have the ability to buy.

From the outside looking in, it is obvious that these low-probability, ugly deals will never close and will divert the salesperson's time and attention from better opportunities. Yet, in spite of the obvious signs, salespeople forge forward, either delusional or oblivious, placing these deals in their pipelines and projections, wasting endless hours working on ugly deals that will never close.

Sadly, the results are predictable. Almost all of these salespeople strike out.

Savvy sales professionals are super disciplined in qualifying prospects. They understand that time is money and it is a waste of time to work with prospects that are not going to buy. They know that qualified buyers are scarce, and a moment spent with a prospect who will never buy takes them away from their most important task, finding prospects that will buy.

It begins with gathering information during prospecting. While setting an appointment is your primary objective with prospects you have already prequalified as potential buyers, gathering information is your primary objective with prospects you have not qualified.

Here's what I mean. If we drew a bell curve from the statistical distribution of qualified prospects in your database/CRM or the potential customers in your market (if you are a start-up and have not yet built a database):

1. A small percentage will be totally qualified and in the buying window (ready for an appointment or ready to buy, in the case of a transactional low-risk product).

2. A larger percentage will be totally qualified—you know the decision maker, the key influencers, the size of the business, the budget, and your competitors. But, they won't be in the buying window due to budget restrictions or contractual obligations.

3. A larger percentage will be semi-qualified—you will have some information, but there will be holes in your data.

4. An even larger percentage will be potential buyers, but you will have almost no information about them or the information will be outdated.

5. A small percentage will never be buyers or will be out of business, or the record in the database will be bogus.

Your drive as a sales professional should always be to spend your time with the most qualified prospects in your database. This means that you will want to:

1. Set appointments with the prospects that are highly qualified and/or in the buying window

2. Nurture the prospects that you've qualified but are not in the buying window

3. Gather information on the prospects for which you have some or no data so you can qualify their potential and learn their buying windows

4. Eliminate the prospect records that are bogus, out of business, too small, too big, or will never be buyers

There are some sales experts who will tell you to set an appointment with every prospect and qualify later. Many are adamant about it. I get their point. They've observed so many salespeople use qualifying as a reason to avoid making calls that they figure the best way to get them to prospect is to have them set appointments and do the qualifying once they're in the meeting.

Frankly it probably makes sense to just set the appointment regardless how qualified your prospect is if:

1. You sell a product or service that is noncontractual

2.There is a high probability that most of your prospects will be buyers because your product is something they use all of the time

3. There is no set budgetary period for making these purchases

4. The decision maker role is fairly consistent and usually a single person

However, when your product or service is complex, contractual (especially when the contract requires exclusivity with a single vendor or limited number of vendors), the sales cycle is long, decision making is done at a high level in the organization, there is a defined budgetary period, or budgets need to be approved in advance, your best bet is to qualify first, then set an appointment.

Define the Strike Zone

The first step in qualifying is to clearly define the strike zone. Far too many companies (especially start-ups and small businesses), sales organizations, and sales professionals fail to develop a profile of a qualified prospect. This includes the optimal time for engaging the prospect prior to the opening of the buying window.

Here is a blinding flash of the obvious: If you don't define the strike zone, you will waste a lot of time chasing ugly deals. This process shouldn't be difficult. If you work for a big company, just go sit down with your sales manager and some of the more successful reps. They'll likely have the information you'll need, decision-making roles, account size, buying windows, budgetary windows, contractual obligations—to build a profile of your ideal opportunity.

If you work for a small company or start-up, start by analyzing your product and service delivery strengths and weaknesses. Look for patterns and commonalities among your best customers. Analyze the deals you are closing and gain a deeper understanding of trigger events that open buying windows. Based on the information you know, gauge how soon you need to engage prior to the buying window opening. Uncover common buyer roles. Then develop a profile of the prospect that is most likely to do business with you and, over the long-term, be a profitable, happy customer.

Once you have developed the profile of your ideal customer, you can develop the questions you'll need to qualify your prospects and identify the best opportunities. Next, make a commitment to measure every prospect, deal, and customer against this profile. When they don't fit, develop the discipline to walk away.

I am not saying that every deal must fit your profile perfectly in order to enter your sales pipe. This is not how the real world works. In some cases, it makes sense to take some risk and swing outside of the strike zone. However, there is a difference in taking a calculated, data-driven risk and chasing an ugly deal.

The end goal is keeping your pipeline full of viable, qualified deals that have a high probability of closing. This is why fanatical prospectors use daily prospecting activity to systematically qualify their databases.

Heed the coachs advice: "Don't swing at nothin' ugly."

Close the Sale

When you are selling transactional, low-risk, or relatively low-cost products or services and prospecting via phone and in-person channels, your primary prospecting objective is closing the sale right on the spot. If you are prospecting via e-mail, text, or social channels, your primary objective is to convert that prospecting touch into a sales conversation that leads to closing the sale.

When closing the sale is your objective, the prospecting interaction gets a bit more complicated because you've got to engage, qualify, and ask them to commit to giving up their time for a sales conversation right on the spot.

On the phone or in person, where you have the highest probability of a one-call close, this means you have to quickly get past the initial reflex response or brush-off, ask one or two questions to qualify the opportunity, and gain agreement for an appointment on the spot that gives you the space to ask deeper questions, bridge to a solution, and close the sale.

It all happens in the span of a few minutes and it requires poise, confidence, and a fundamental mastery of the sales process.

The techniques for closing the sale on a prospecting call (one call close) are beyond the scope of this book. However, we'll discuss the techniques you'll need to get past the initial pushback and objections from your prospect and move them into a sales conversation.

Build Familiarity

Our data that we've gathered and analyzed from a diverse set of sources indicate that it takes, on average:

1. 1 to 3 touches to reengage an inactive customer

2. 1 to 5 touches to engage a prospect who is in the buying window and is familiar with you and your brand

3. 3 to 10 touches to engage a prospect who has a high degree of familiarity with you or your brand, but is not in the buying window

4. 5 to 12 touches to engage a warm inbound lead

5. 5 to 20 touches to engage a prospect who has some familiarity with you and your brand—buying window dependent

6. 20 to 50 touches to engage a cold prospect who does not know you or your brand

These are general averages. Depending on your overall brand recognition, geographic location, prospecting channel, product, service, sales cycle, and industry vertical, you may find that these numbers shift in or out of your favor.

The point, however, is not the numbers. It is the story these numbers tell us. Familiarity plays an important role in getting prospects to engage. The more familiar a prospect is with you, your brand, and/or your company, the more likely they will be willing to accept and return your calls, reply to your e-mails, accept a social media connection request, respond to a text message, and engage when you are prospecting in person.

Building familiarity is almost always a secondary or tertiary objective of a prospecting touch, though at times, especially with strategic prospecting campaigns, it may be your primary objective. Familiarity as a prospecting objective requires a long-term focus because it is improved through the cumulative impact of ongoing prospecting activity. This is why savvy sales professionals create strategic prospecting campaigns (SPCs) that cross-leverage prospecting channels to systematically build familiarity.

For example, let's say you have done some research and uncovered the contact names of 100 manufacturing operations managers—the most likely decision makers for your service. Problem is, they don't know you and you don't know them. Many of them may have no familiarity with your company.

In this scenario, it may take multiple touches over a long period of time to get one of these potential buyers to engage. To gain their attention you might develop an SPC that includes phone calls and voice mails, e-mail, social, targeted trade shows, and industry conferences. Your primary objective is to create enough familiarity that these cold prospects are more likely to engage.

1. Each time you leave a voice mail, they hear your name and your company name and their familiarity with you increases.

2. Each time you send an e-mail, they read your name and see your e-mail address, company name, and service brand, and their familiarity with you increases.

3. When you connect with them on LinkedIn, familiarity increases.

4. When you like, comment on, or share something they post on a social media channel, familiarity increases.

5. When you meet them at an industry conference and put a face with a name, familiarity increases.

The bottom line is, if you don't have a plan and you don't know your objectives, your prospecting blocks will be far less effective and you will waste time. However, when you build more effective prospecting lists, with clear objectives, centered on specific prospecting channels, your prospecting blocks are easier, faster, more impactful, and generate far better results.

CHAPTER 2:

HOW TO IDENTIFY THE IDEAL B2B CUSTOMER

Finding the right customers can be like looking for love. Where should you look? Who should you pursue? What are the best strategies?

There are plenty of marketers who pursue the "Dive Bar" strategy of lead generation. They'll get phone numbers at any time, from anyone and everyone, and pass on these unqualified leads-on-cocktail-napkins to their sales team in the hopes that one or two might actually become a customer "love connection." But what really happens is that your salesperson goes on a cold-calling binge and ends up hating himself in the morning, leaving you, his Marketing BFF, feeling as though you should have done something differently. Perhaps you should have set him up with nicer, more respectable leads. The kind you might meet at your grandma's church picnic. Don't stoop to this level. Be intelligent about your search, and know when to forego those less-than-ideal opportunities. Don't just throw yourself at every lead that walks by. Your company deserves better than a dive bar.

Profiling Your Ideal Customer

Start your search by devising an ideal customer profile. Who would your dream customer be? What qualities would they need to have to make your business relationship work for the long haul? What are their needs, and how can you satisfy them? Just as being choosy with your prospective dates can yield huge relationship dividends later on, so can scoring and grading leads help you to separate the wheat from the chaff and pursue those prospects that would make the most ideal customers.

But in order to make this approach work for you, your sales and marketing teams will need to achieve both clarity and consensus on the type of customers your company wants to attract. This essential first step requires marketers to collaborate with their salespeople, the ones who are out there on the front lines every day.

The following questions will get you started on developing that ideal customer profile:

• What size of organization would you prefer to deal with? On average, how many employees would it have?

• In which geographic areas would you prefer that these organizations be located?

• In which market sectors or industry verticals would these organizations operate?

• What are the most likely job titles of the individuals who would be making buying decisions?

• What other positions in the organization might be involved in buying decisions?

Encourage your sales staff to think out loud about their most successful sales and best customers. Ask them to consider the following questions:

• Which existing customers were the easiest and quickest to convert?

• What similarities do these customers possess?

• Are there any specific criteria that would make prospects an especially good fit?

Once your marketing and sales teams have agreed upon an ideal customer profile, don't stop there. Publish and circulate it so that everyone stays focused on your goals. Review and revise your definition to incorporate real-life experiences with prospects.

Having a clearly defined profile of your ideal customer is the absolute starting point for determining which lead generation strategies work best for you and for improving the effectiveness of your marketing initiatives. You may also discover that once you've begun attracting more targeted customers, asking for referrals becomes easier and generates better responses, since you've started by providing a more precise specification of what you're looking for. With your thinking now distilled and concentrated, your marketing strategies will start to take on real definition and direction.

Grading

Before assigning leads, your lead qualification or marketing operations team should grade them according to how well they fit your ideal customer profile; this will help your sales reps properly prioritize them. Most lead grading systems start with a default profile that you can customize by setting your preferred criteria (location, company size, job title, etc.) for qualifying prospects You can also create any additional profiles that meet your company's needs, and you can use multiple profiles if you want to target several different audiences. For example, you may have different profiles, and perhaps different grading criteria, for your technical prospects as opposed to executive prospects.

Selecting Your Grading Criteria

When evaluating inbound leads to send to the sales team, lead scoring and grading work together to help you determine your ideal prospects. While scoring happens automatically, without any real setup required unless you want to fine tune it with additional personalization, setting up a grading profile is a bit more of an art. Since grading is designed to help you determine how well a prospect fits your organization, you might want to personalize your criteria beyond the defaults provided by your solution. Sales and marketing should collaborate to come up with a set of acceptable criteria that will help them arrive at a unified vision of what constitutes a good lead.

Sales Lead Insights put together a list of potential grading criteria frequently used in the industry to help you build your own grading profile. Here are some of the suggestions:

• Consider both firmographics (items relating to a target company, like industry or company size) and demographics (items relating to a specific person, like job title).

• Consider the prospect's role in the purchasing decision.

• Consider the fit. Does your product meet or exceed their requirements?

• Consider the prospect's available budget.

• Consider the revenue potential of the deal.

Some of these criteria may be immediately obvious, and they're great candidates for automation based on information collected on forms. Other items that are initially unknowns, like budget and timeline, may become more clearly defined once a sales rep has made contact. Though not as applicable to the sales handoff, it is still beneficial to update the grading criteria as you learn more about a prospect. This will help the sales team prioritize follow-up calls, and it allows both teams to start tracking overall trends.

Defining Grades

Grades are based on explicit information about the prospect, whereas scores (discussed below) are based on implicit activities performed. Prospects with grades of A+ or A are considered a great fit, while those with grades of A-, B+, or B are a good fit, and those graded B-, C+, or C constitute just average fits. Some grading systems can be configured to automatically confer a certain grade on a prospect based on specific attributes, such as belonging to the industry vertical in which your company specializes.

The letter grade assigned to a prospect corresponds with how closely that prospect fits the ideal customer profile, as well as how qualified that customer is according to the criteria you've set. It is advantageous to incorporate a methodology for how grading works in your organization, based on your own custom profiles. For example, when prospect information matches certain desired values, you could adjust grades as follows:

Industry – increase/decrease by a partial grade

Department – increase/decrease by a partial grade

Job title – increase/decrease by a partial grade

Company size – increase/decrease by a partial grade

Location – increase/decrease by a partial grade

Again, it is important to develop a process specific to your organization. Grading can be automated through the use of automation rules, which make grade adjustments based on criteria that you specify. For example, if you wanted to target company vice-presidents as potential decision-makers, you could set up a rule that would place any prospects with this job title into a list that receives emails targeted at executive-level decision-makers. The myriad other uses for automation rules will be discussed in subsequent sections.

Scoring

While grading is based on explicit objective information about a prospect, scoring is based on actions taken by the prospect. Lead scoring adds points for every action that a prospect performs on your website or in response to an email or some other call to action. A prospect can earn points towards their total score by browsing the website, clicking on the link in an email, downloading a white paper, signing up for a webinar, or filling out a web form. You can customize the number of points awarded for particular activities, and you can decide which activities accrue points. For example, simply landing on your page may add only a single point to a prospect's score, but a prospect who enters —pricing‖ in an internal site search may get 10 points, since this action is a far better indicator of purchasing intent.

Here's an example of what a default points system for prospect scoring might look like:

Successful completion of a form = +50 points

Site search query = +3 points

Tracked link click = +3 points

Hosted file access = +3 points

Visitor session = +3 points

Visitor page view = +1 point

Form/form handler/landing page error = -5 points

CRM opportunity created = +50 points

CRM opportunity lost = -100 points

Prospect scores can also be modified by automation rules. For example, an automation rule might be set up so that if the prospects have requested a demo or a particular white paper, 50 bonus points will be added to their scores. You could elect to give 50 points for all form submissions but award a "bonus" to a form or landing page submission that shows a more serious intent (such as filling out a form requesting a free trial). Automation rules can handle all of this behind the scenes. Rules can also be used to give negative points in order to downgrade certain prospects, such as a competitor's employee who is visiting your site purely for investigative purposes.

Customize by Page

Some marketing automation solutions allow you to customize scoring by page, enabling you to add or subtract points based on prospect activities on the individual page level. This would not typically be done on every page, but only on important pages, such as a pricing page or another page that conveys a similar degree of intent. Tracking codes can be also used to give negative points (or subtract points) on, for example, a site's "Careers" page, since the visitor is most likely interested in a job as opposed to your product or service.

Lead Assignment

Marketing automation solutions allow you to automatically assign leads to sales reps when they reach a certain grade and score criteria. Automatic assignments can be done based on a variety of different actors including geographic territories, type of organization, and industry vertical. For example, you could set your preferences to automatically assign all prospects with a country value of Canada, United States, or Mexico to your North American sales representative. Some organizations automatically nurture leads until they reach a specific grade and score threshold. At that point, qualified leads are assigned via a round-robin system to the next available sales rep for follow up. This system allows for a timely and equitable distribution of only sales-ready leads. Some marketing automation solutions can be configured to send out regular updates to sales reps to notify them of new prospect activity on their site within a given timeframe, which helps reps prioritize their efforts and better allocate their time.

Connecting The Dots

Connectors are add-on tools that enable marketing automation platforms to sync with third-party applications such as a CRM system or Google AdWords. Data can be passed back and forth between the two applications, allowing a user to easily manage many formerly disparate marketing channels and tools from within a single interface. Connectors provide the essential links needed to sync your own prospect data with external information you collect from various sites and applications. Connecting the dots between these scattered bits of valuable data can help you get a more complete picture of your prospects and their tastes and motivations, maximizing the efficiency of your marketing automation activities and thereby enabling you to better address prospects' needs with the appropriate solutions. The following examples illustrate the types of information that can be shared through connectors.

CRM Connectors

Integrating a marketing automation solution with a CRM system continuously syncs data between the two platforms and allows the sales team to view updated information on prospect activity from within the CRM system. The contact database in the CRM can be sorted by the scores and grades assigned by the marketing automation platform, for example. The continuous sync between the two platforms ensures that data is non-redundant and always up-to-date. Integration with familiar systems also means fewer barriers to company-wide adoption and easier day-to-day use. Most marketing automation solutions offer native integrations with CRMs like salesforce.com, NetSuite, SugarCRM, and Microsoft Dynamics, but others can be integrated via a web service API.

Other Connectors

Google AdWords is a pay per click (PPC) advertising medium that allows you to create ads based on keywords or phrases related to your business. Marketing automation solutions can hook into your Google AdWords account and track prospects who reach you through this type of paid search. You can tie cost data from AdWords to opportunity data from your CRM to determine your true cost per qualified lead and search engine marketing ROI.

Google Analytics is an enterprise-class web analytics solution that lets you view and analyze your traffic data. A Google Analytics connector is designed to simplify the flow of information between Google Analytics, your marketing automation platform, and your CRM system. Such a connector enables users of Google Analytics Keyword Tags in URLs to pass those tags into a connected marketing automation platform. Once the tags are set up, the fields can be synced with a compatible CRM system, allowing you to use the CRM reporting features to run custom analysis on your tags.

Data can be collected from all five of the Google Analytics tags: source, medium, term, content, and name. You could also utilize the connector to create a new campaign based on your Google Analytics campaign tag for any new prospects coming in from tagged URLs.

LinkedIn is best known for its networking capabilities, but it is also a great way to generate leads with the most potential. A great advantage of LinkedIn for finding new prospects is that it allows you to see profiles of people with whom you are not directly connected. This feature lets you look at different people within an organization and choose the ones you'd like to reach out to based on their position and fit with your company's offerings. One particularly useful feature on LinkedIn is the "Get introduced through a connection" option, which allows you to ask a mutual connection to introduce you to a prospect. This option greatly improves your chances of making contact with a prospect because the request is not random or anonymous. Marketing automation solutions that connect to LinkedIn enable you to easily augment prospect profiles by checking out their professional credentials and connections.

Jigsaw (owned by salesforce.com) is another prospecting tool used by sales professionals and marketers to get fresh and accurate sales leads and business contact information. It boasts detailed contact information for over 19 million people. Jigsaw can be connected to a marketing automation platform so that its internal information on your prospects can be easily accessed within your marketing automation platform. Twilio is a web service API that helps you instantly follow up with interested prospects by phone. This type of pay-as- you-go telephony application can be tremendously useful when used in conjunction with certain features of a marketing automation platform. Twilio can be set up so that when a prospect fills out a form on your website, the assigned sales rep will immediately receive a phone call from the computer which reads out the prospect's information. Cold calling might not be easy, but most salespeople love picking up a ringing phone. What's more is that the advantage of being able to follow up when your product or solution is top of mind for a prospect is invaluable for salespeople.

Twitter was originally intended for use by individuals, but companies are increasingly utilizing it as a marketing and promotional channel. Most marketing automation platforms allow you to tie a Twitter username to a prospect so that their most recent tweets can be easily viewed within the platform. Tweets can provide insight into a prospect's thought process and may provide clues as to their needs or specific pain points you could address when you make contact.

Desktop alert applications provide sales and marketing teams with real-time alerts of visitor and prospect activity. Results refresh periodically to indicate whether visitors have taken specific actions on your company's website. Some marketing automation solutions offer these as a standalone add-on application.

Connectors like the ones described here are valuable tools offered by some marketing automation solutions. Once you've run through a quick setup, connectors make prospect information from the connected applications instantly available in the marketing automation platform's interface. Because connectors help you collect additional information to round out prospect profiles, they make your marketing efforts more effective while greatly enhancing communication with prospects.

Social Media

Social media tools provide inexpensive, broad-based channels for lead generation and qualification. They draw users to your website and push your content through their own spheres of influence. While social media channels can require a sizeable commitment of time and attention, it's an investment that can really pay off.

Community Marketing

A specialized type of social marketing called community marketing is typically a corporate-sponsored forum where customers and prospects interact to share feedback about product features and performance. Community marketing has opened up new opportunities for companies to improve their brands through sharing best practices and soliciting candid feedback. Community marketing channels are sometimes referred to as Web 2.0 applications because they depend on user-generated content and allow users to interact with, add to, or change content. This interaction can take the form of idea exchanges, forums and message boards, wikis, blogs, rating systems, videos, opinion polls, and shared reviews, all of which collect customer opinions and drive increased sales through a more viral approach to marketing.

The challenge that lies in community marketing is the policing of inappropriate comments and inaccurate content. Fortunately there are various monitoring mechanisms, such as required customer registrations and comment approval, that keep contributions in check and maintain the integrity of the content. As with social media channels, community marketing requires a significant investment in time and attention before it can be used effectively. But when managed well, community marketing can be an extremely economical and effective way to build your brand and boost your business.

Real Results, Real Quick

These are all great suggestions for customer profiling, scoring and grading leads, and connecting your marketing automation solution to third-party applications. But how hard is it to get both sales and marketing departments on board and cooperating to implement these suggestions? How long does it actually take to see a real return on these strategies?

Believe it or not, it's really not as hard as it sounds. Selecting a good marketing automation solution is the first step in the process. Once you've implemented the solution and adopted the suggestions discussed above, you'll see results almost immediately.

When a company called Omnipress decided to adopt a marketing automation solution, not only did they achieve their desired results, but they got those results far faster than initially expected. Omnipress offers a "one-stop-shop" solution for producing conference and educational meeting materials in print, digital media, and online formats. Each year, more than 800 associations, meeting professionals, and volunteers trust Omnipress to complete their projects. Omnipress had already developed a robust multichannel marketing plan with an emphasis on providing frequent, compelling content. They were using some programs that provided high-level metrics, but they still lacked in-depth, detailed information about individual visitors. In addition, the marketing team had no established way of passing their findings to their sales team.

Omnipress saw results within just two months of implementing a marketing automation solution. The return far exceeded their expectations. Some of their most noteworthy successes are outlined below:

• Omnipress generated 517% more leads year over year after the adoption of a marketing automation solution.

• They were able to better target the needs of new leads while also gaining valuable insight into the interests, needs, and upgrade potential of current customers.

• Sales reps completely altered their selling approach to one that rarely required cold calling prospects who hadn't already visited the Omnipress website to learn about the company.

• Omnipress kept costs down by using their marketing automation solution to increase incoming leads and to refocus current leads without having to attend expensive trade shows or hire additional sales staff.

If you're willing to abandon the 'Dive Bar' approach to lead generation and begin concentrating on quality over quantity, you'll discover that this methodology makes the most of both your marketing and sales assets. If you can create an informed and consistent means of grading and scoring your prospects, coupled with a fair and systematic method of lead assignment, you'll have taken the first big step toward bridging that gap between these notoriously at- odds departments. You'll also find that augmenting your own prospect data with information from outside sources via connectors will greatly enhance the quality of the leads that get passed along to your sales team. A good marketing automation solution with appropriate features makes all of these processes a piece of cake.

CHAPTER 3:

STAY CONNECTED TO NON-SALES READY LEADS

Once you've profiled your ideal customer and started scoring and grading leads for fit and relevance, you'll find you're getting far better matches for your sales team. Now the true courtship can begin. Unfortunately, in today's B2B sales cycle, that courtship can often be long and complicated, and there are lots of opportunities to lose touch along the way.

It's common knowledge that the majority of viable sales leads end up slipping through the cracks. One source suggests that 79% of leads don't get any follow-up from sales because they're perceived to be of below-average quality. Oftentimes, leads that aren't yet ready to buy are dismissed as unviable. But as B2B lead generation experts have pointed out, with the proper nurturing, as many as 45% of these neglected leads can become sales-ready within just 12 months. Without a system in place to facilitate quick and consistent follow-up, marketers and salespeople unintentionally allow these leads to disappear into a black hole. So what can you do to make sure your company doesn't succumb to these statistics?

Lead Nurturing.

A good marketing automation solution allows you to place non-sales-ready leads into nurturing tracks. You can then ensure that your marketing efforts periodically "touch" them via automated, timed, one-to-one email messages. All links and calls to action in your marketing collateral are tracked individually to prospects, and your sales reps will be notified as soon as a lead responds. By automating the lead nurturing process, you are not only further qualifying your leads, but also freeing up sales or marketing personnel who formerly did this task manually. For your lead nurturing efforts to produce the best results, however, you need to reach out to your prospects in ways that are both sustained and timely. In other words, your lead nurturing campaign touches must happen over time and on tie.

Over Time: Drip Marketing.

Drip marketing is a lead nurturing strategy that involves periodically sending out helpful information and relevant promotions to prospects and/or clients. The phrase drip marketing is evocative of drip irrigation, the agricultural process of watering plants or crops using small amounts of water over an extended period of time. The idea behind the concept of drip marketing is the "Law of 29", a marketing axiom stating that the average prospect must view a marketing message at least 29 times before they will become a client. While the Law of 29 might not apply in every situation, it is always a good idea to stay in touch with prospects and clients to help build a sustainable working relationship for the long haul. Drip marketing isn't really about selling—it's about building the kind of relationship that will lead to sales down the road.

Get Strategic

The best thing about drip marketing is that it runs itself. Once you put it in place, you don't have to worry about it anymore. Drip marketing does require a plan of action, but you can coordinate with and complement your existing efforts by creating a drip marketing plan that's consistent with your general marketing strategy.

The ideal time to develop drip marketing campaigns is while planning your yearly marketing calendar. Try to send out something at least monthly to keep your name in front of current and prospective clients. Your communications with each group might be different, however. For example, prospects need periodic bits of helpful information that will nudge them to make a buying decision, while current clients should be informed of relevant news such as feature improvements or upgrade opportunities.

Think ahead about possible opportunities for reaching out to prospects and customers in the coming year. These opportunities exist through a wide range of avenues, such as extending invitations to company-sponsored events, passing along industry-specific news, or sharing coverage of your company's annual community outreach activities. For example, you already know months in advance when and where your annual trade show or users conference will take place. Make sure your customers and prospects get an invitation well in advance of the event, followed by timely reminders sent out periodically on a drip program. Marketing automation tools let you create and execute the components of campaigns like these ahead of time so that you'll have more free time to work on fine-tuning other aspects of your marketing strategy.

Tone and substance

The fundamental underpinnings of any great email campaign the Four T's (Tailoring, Testing, Timing, Tracking) also apply to drip marketing. However, since the goal is not selling but keeping in touch, drip campaigns will be appreciably different in tone and substance. These qualitative differences are reflected in the following collection of best practices for drip marketing.

1. Drop the hard sell.

Think of drip marketing items as the Hallmark cards of your marketing toolkit. They're like friendly little notes to remind your prospects and customers that you're thinking of them, that you're keeping their needs in mind, or that you just want to check in to see how they're doing. These greetings can be even more impressive if you're able to tie them to more personal customer interactions by offering holiday greetings, congratulatory wishes at the end of the quarter, or thank-you messages on the anniversary of their signed purchase or service agreement. Sales reps can sign their own communications and, if they wish, include a personal message: "Hi John, I saw this article and thought you might be interested."

Marketing automation tools enable this kind of individualized approach through easy personalization of your communications with prospects and customers. Ongoing friendly contact will eventually forge a good working relationship with prospects so that you can drop the hard sell and focus on guiding them to make the buying decision that's in their best interest.

2. Get permission.

Back when it passed the CAN-SPAM Act was jokingly referred to as the, You Can Spam, law. Indeed, many marketers have interpreted it as precisely that—an excuse to send out unsolicited email communications without permission. To comply with the CAN-SPAM Act, marketers need not obtain explicit permission from their intended recipients; there are other ways to comply with the letter, if not the spirit, of the legislation. For years marketers have been using the "negative opt-in" strategy as an effective method for gaining a recipient's unwitting permission to be sent a barrage of emails. This tactic buries a conveniently pre-checked checkbox somewhere on a webpage or in an email. The hope is that the recipient will overlook the checkbox's accompanying language, which effectively grants their "permission" to be emailed in the future.

Such questionable tactics might work in the short term, but in the long run, they will only damage your reputation and undermine your marketing message. If you're serious about relationship marketing, don't even consider taking the covert approach to obtaining permission. Make sure your prospects are only getting emails that they actually want to receive.

3. Send presents.

Just as any human courtship can be sweetened by the occasional bouquet of flowers or little memento, so can customer relationships. Marketing automation solutions make it easy to deliver genuine value in your communications by making presents of your presence. You need only ensure that your message is useful, unique, and not blatantly promotional.

Opportunities for clever gift-giving are limited only by the imagination. Nurturing emails can include links to short customer testimonial videos and case studies; articles, reports, and white papers; industry-related news or relevant third-party information; and, best of all, freebies such as basic consulting services, free sample chapters of your upcoming book, special product sneak previews, or helpful proprietary tips and tricks.

4. Balance variety and consistency.

You definitely want prospects to recognize your brand and to identify with your marketing slogans, but you don't want to become boring, redundant, or irrelevant. There's some truth in that old saw about familiarity breeding contempt. Your brand can be consistent from drip to drip without making your prospect think,"Didn't I just see this last week?" Blasting away at your prospects with duplicate emails, or emails that are so similar as to seem like duplicates, is not marketing—it's harassment.

5. Segment your lists.

If you interact with different types of prospects, think about their specific needs and interests and make your messaging relevant. This kind of specialization will most likely require using more than one nurturing track. You could decide to segment your leads based on any number of distinguishing factors, such as a prospect's job title or industry, or the products in which they're interested. Then make sure to follow up with targeted content that each grouping of prospects will find relevant or beneficial. Using rules features in your marketing automation platform makes it easy to create segmented nurturing lists.

6. Be patient (but not lazy).

Teach your sales team to be patient—but not lazy. Drip marketing is a great tool to keep your company and product top of mind with prospects, but it can't take the place of traditional sales calls. Conversely, your sales team has to let marketing plant the seed and build the relationship before they send a sales rep in with guns blazing.

The bottom line? Leads that aren't ready to buy don't want to talk to salespeople. That's why drip marketing is such a powerful tool. There are plenty of sales opportunities out there, and each one can take months to develop. Rather than having the sales team jump on every opportunity with equal vigor, you should task your marketing team with passing on only the most sales-ready leads. The remaining prospects should be nurtured, slowly but surely, until they're ready to buy.

Many B2B products and services are complex, requiring potential clients to do a significant amount of research before they're ready to buy. Drip marketing is a great way to do this, because marketers can customize the information that each lead receives, making sure that this information is sent out at regular intervals. Obviously, drip marketing can do most of the heavy lifting for you here, but always keep in mind that trying to sell to leads too early in the sales cycle is risky and usually ends up being counterproductive since nobody wants to feel like they're being pushed to buy before they're ready. On the other hand, having the sales team manually nurture leads is a waste of time. Salespeople should be able to spend their time doing what they do best: selling the product to leads that already know what your product is about, and persuading these leads that your product is the best fit for their needs. Drip marketing lets the sales team concentrate on selling by ensuring that marketing is creating high-quality leads that are both a good fit and are ready to buy.

One of the key benefits of marketing automation is the coordination it fosters between sales and marketing teams. This kind of teamwork is critical to creating a seamless sales cycle that begins with a carefully designed marketing strategy (including drip marketing campaigns) and ends with a salesperson closing the deal. Because drip marketing isn't about hard selling, it doesn't make the sale on its own. However, it helps build a positive relationship with prospects, who are then nurtured until they're ready to buy.

7. Think outside the inbox.

Drip emails are the backbone of any drip marketing strategy, but there are other ways to communicate in the context of a drip campaign. Other options for making regular contact with your prospects include sending handwritten notes, leaving unintrusive voicemails, and making the most of social media outlets for periodic messages.

8. Don't leave customers behind.

Just because some of your leads haven't been converted into opportunities yet doesn't mean that they have no value. In fact, some of them might just be waiting to hear from you. Setting up a drip marketing program specifically designed with old leads in mind will ensure that even if your sales reps don't stay in touch, your nurturing efforts will. Whatever happened to that lead who dropped off the radar because a sales rep wasn't able to make contact? What about those unconverted website visitors who signed up for a webinar but never showed up? You were once top of mind for these prospects. At some point, you did something right that got their attention. Don't sacrifice the hard work you've already invested and the relationship you've started to develop with them. Marketing automation tools make it easy and economical to reengage these leads, and when the time comes, drip marketing can greatly reduce the time that sales reps must spend in reiterating the benefits of your product or service. Maintaining constant contact means that potential customers won't slip through the cracks.

On Time: Responsive Marketing

Lead nurturing requires a special sense of timing. To market responsively, you need to consider the experience of the typical recipient who joins your list, signs up for that first webinar, or otherwise enters into a relationship with your company. What will the significant milestones in that emerging relationship be? And how at each milestone can you best respond both rapidly and appropriately?

The emerging customer relationship actually takes shape much as a dating relationship would. From the point of introduction, the relationship progresses, sometimes slowly, sometimes quickly, through the initial, getting acquainted, stage before finally maturing into a committed relationship built on trust. In the context of today's complex sales cycle, that progress might not always be as fast or linear as expected, but marketing technology tools can help you keep in touch throughout the entire process, ensuring that your budding relationship with a prospective customer ever lapses or breaks down.

The introduction

The original touchpoint in any relationship is the initial meeting—that one chance you have to make a good first impression. The welcome message is probably the most widely read email in any given drip program, and it's crucial in that it comes at a time when new subscribers have recently become acquainted with your company or product and are highly receptive to receiving your message. Yet many marketers still manage to miss this golden opportunity to say Hello, Welcome, or It's nice to meet you. A benchmark study published in 2019 found some surprising results. Out of 112 of the largest online retailers surveyed:

•Only 76% sent out welcome emails

•23% took longer than 24 hours to send out a welcome message after subscribers signed up

•Only 76% explained the benefits of being a subscriber

•Only 87% included a link to their homepage.

It's mystifying that so many marketers still manage to botch, or completely miss out on, this once-in-a-business-relationship opportunity, particularly since welcome emails typically generate substantial open and click-through rates. Marketing automation tools can be invaluable in helping you nail this decisive opportunity for each and every prospect you come in contact with.

Welcome emails can set expectations by informing recipients of what they might encounter in future messages. They can be designed as one or two simple messages, or a series of notifications. They should be tailored to reflect the specific nature of your introduction; for example, prospects who sign up to receive a newsletter should be thanked specifically for doing so, while those who join an online user community should get a customized Welcome to our community! -type message. If your introduction has been through a referral, this should be acknowledged, and the prospect should be placed in the appropriate campaign. The bottom line is that any campaign strategy needs to recognize, and accord the proper respect to, that all- important first meeting. First impressions are important. It's critical to get things right the first time, or there might not be a second time.

Getting acquainted

In the middle stage of a developing relationship, the two parties are getting to know one another. You've learned something about your new prospect from information he or she has voluntarily provided, and your lead scoring and grading tools are working behind the scenes to gauge their fit and their interest level based on their activities online. But your prospect is learning about you in this stage, too. When prospects are in exploratory mode, they are seeking information, evaluating your products or services against those of your competitors, and absorbing cues about how you might treat them in an established customer relationship. This intermediate stage is brimming with opportunities for educating prospects, building personal relationships, and gently nudging prospects toward that all- important commitment: the sale.

For a drip marketing campaign to be really effective at this stage, it needs to respond rapidly to every overture your prospect makes, and every response should be as relevant as possible. It is at this stage that you can most effectively employ marketing automation tools for prospect nurturing. Using tracking clues from a prospect's online activity, you can engineer your communications to deliver information with increasing relevancy based on where he or she is in the buying process. This can be especially important with regard to big-ticket items that require many weeks or months of research on the part of potential buyers. B2B marketing strategist Ardath Albee recommends creating a storyline to help keep marketing content consistently tied to your main message. This involves creating personas for your most ideal prospect segments and then building a storyline for each persona, detailing possible routes to purchase for each product or solution so that you can map content to buying stages. The goal is to deliver a continuous flow of content that matches up to prospect needs from the start.

This approach obviously requires more forethought and planning than just the basic drip marketing approach of sending content over time. It implies the creation of a more complex rule structure within your marketing automation platform, which requires you to develop a repository of generic content to send off at each stage of the buying process. Having a marketing automation solution in place simplifies this complex task by letting you craft a conceptually sophisticated plan that can be implemented simply and automatically. For example, a request for a white paper can be acknowledged by an autoresponder email that supplies the appropriate link. If the prospect does not click the white paper link in the email, a follow-up email is automatically sent two days later with a note asking if they've had a chance to read the white paper and providing a link to see it again. This process can be repeated every so often, but with related white papers, case studies, or other relevant material. You'll be able to monitor prospect responses throughout this entire process so that sales reps will be able to swiftly respond to prospect needs with appropriate personal attention.

It's not over yet

In the third stage of building a customer relationship, you and your prospect are now a team—you've committed to working together and have officially become an item. Now that your prospect is a customer, it might seem like the relationship has ended, or perhaps that it more properly belongs to service and support. But this is not the time for marketing to quietly slip out of the room. As drip marketing expert Lori Feldman has pointed out, new customers can often suffer from buyer's remorse. It's just human nature for customers to wonder if maybe, just maybe, they should have shopped around a little more, negotiated harder for a better deal, or asked a few more questions. That's a disconnect, Feldman says, and the only way to fix it is to overload a new customer with personalized attention through an automated onboarding process. This is a great idea, not only because it continues to nurture the customer, but also because it adds ongoing value to the relationship by ensuring that your new customer has everything they need to succeed with your company—and, by extension, no nagging regrets.

The sold, customer shouldn't be forgotten or written off simply as an opportunity marked as "won" in the CRM. Current customers are often sources of repeat business or referrals, so it's crucial to maintain a good relationship with them even after the initial deal has been closed. Even if your customers are not especially susceptible to up-selling or cross-selling, it always pays to cultivate references and advocates—someone who feels so positively about your company and their experience with your product or service that they're willing to provide great references for future customers. What do satisfied customers typically do when they have a great experience? They tell their friends and colleagues. The huge payoff of a drip campaign that stays in touch with satisfied customers beyond the final stage of the buying cycle is more than worth the minimal effort it takes to set it up within your marketing automation platform.

There are plenty of chances at this stage to say thank you, something that few companies really take the time to do for their customers, as well as many opportunities for follow-up campaign items. Just as you wouldn't miss the opportunity to follow up after a great date or business meeting, you don't want to squander the chance to send a direct response to a prospect who has downloaded a white paper, participated in a webinar, watched a demonstration, or signed up for a free trial. Automated email campaigns can also be used to supplement any follow-up calls by sales reps during this end stage.

A Final Word On Drip Marketing

The goals of a drip marketing campaign can extend beyond lead nurturing to provide additional value to your marketing team. The resultant outcomes can be not only specific, but also measurable. Email open, click-through, and opt-out rates are some examples of useful drip marketing metrics. You can look at these early-stage metrics, in addition to late-stage ones such as time to purchase and purchase frequency, in order to get an idea of how effective your drip marketing campaigns are and to calculate ROI for specific tools.

Setting up a drip marketing campaign requires an initial commitment of time and planning, but this investment pays off many times over. According to marketing research firm Forrester Research, companies that excel at drip marketing raise their win rates by 7% and have sales representatives who make quota 9% more often. Additionally, prospects and customers who receive drip marketing messages buy more, require less discounting, and have shorter sales cycles than those who were not part of a drip campaign.18 In today's business climate, even modest improvements like these can constitute an important competitive edge. If you're not leveraging marketing automation tools to keep prospects and customers engaged through carefully crafted lead nurturing efforts, you're effectively leaving revenue on the table.

CHAPTER 4:

HOW TO INCREASE LANDING PAGE CONVERSION RATES

There's lots of buzz about blogging, viral marketing, social networking, and other new methods of generating eyeballs and traffic online. But all that traffic won't make you any money unless you can convert those unique visitors to leads or customers. Depending on whether you are selling a product directly from your landing page, asking visitors to download a free white paper, or promoting a Webinar or demonstration, conversion rates can range from as low as one percent or less to as much as 50 percent or more. Here are 10 keys to writing landing pages that maximize online conversion rates:

1. **Build credibility early.**

People have always been skeptical of advertising, and with the proliferation of SPAM and shady operators, they are even more skeptical of what they read online. Therefore, your landing page copy must immediately overcome that skepticism.

One way to do that is to make sure one or more "credibility builders" are clearly displayed on the first screen the visitor sees. In the banner at the top of the page, use your logo and company name if you are well known; universities, associations, and other institutions can place their official seal in the upper left of the screen.

Within or immediately under the banner, put a strong testimonial. Consider adding a pre-head or subhead which summarizes the company's mission statement or credentials. At www.bnasoftware.com, the positioning statement is: "Expert Software for a New Level of Efficiency and Control".

2. Capture the e-mail addresses of non-buyers.

There are a number of mechanisms available for capturing the e-mail address of visitors who click on your landing page but do not buy the product. One is to use a window with copy offering a free report or e-course in exchange for submitting an e-mail address. This window can be served to the visitor as a pop-up (it appears when the visitor arrives at the landing page) or a pop-under (a window that appears when the visitor attempts to leave the landing page without making an inquiry or purchase). These are both blocked by pop-up blockers. A "floater" is a window that slides onto the screen from the side or top. Unlike the pop-up and pop-under, the floater is part of the Website HTML code, so it is not stopped by the pop-up blocker.

3. Use lots of testimonials.

Testimonials build credibility and overcome skepticism, as do case studies and white papers posted on the Website. If you invite customers to a live event, ask if they would be willing to give you a brief testimonial recorded on video. Have a professional videographer tape it, get a signed release from the customer, and post the testimonial on your website as a streaming video that require the customer to click a button to hear the testimonial, rather than have the video play automatically when the visitor clicks on the page.

For written testimonials, customers may suggest that you write what you want them to say and just run it by them for approval. Politely ask that they give you their opinion of your product in their own words instead of having you do it. Reason: what they come up with will likely be more specific, believable, and detailed than your version, which might smack of puffery and promotion.

4. **Use lots of bullets.**

Highlight key features and benefits in a list of short, easy-to-read bulleted items. I often use a format where the first part of the bullet is the feature, and after a dash comes the benefit; e.g., "Quick-release adhesive system – your graphics stay clean and don't stick together." Online buyers like to think they are getting a lot for their money, so when selling a product directly from your landing page, be sure all major features and important benefits are covered in a comprehensive bullet list appearing on your landing page.

When generating leads by giving away white papers, you don't need a huge list of bulleted features and benefits. But using bullets to describe the contents of the paper and the benefits that information delivers can raise conversion rates for download requests.

5. **Arouse curiosity in the headline.**

The headline should arouse curiosity, make a powerful promise, or otherwise grab the reader's attention so he has no choice but to keep reading. The headline for a landing page selling a training program on how to become a professional property locator makes a big promise: "Become a Property Locator Today – and Make $100,000 a Year in the Greatest Real Estate Career That Only a Few Insiders Know About."

6. **Use a conversational copy style.**

Most corporate Websites are unemotional and sterile: just "information." But a landing page is a letter from one human being to another. Make it sound that way. Even if your product is highly technical and you are selling it to techies, remember that they are still human beings, and you cannot sell something by boring people to death.

7. Incorporate an emotional hook in the headline and lead paragraph.

Logical selling can work, but tapping into the prospect's emotions is much stronger especially when you correctly assess how the prospect is feeling about your product or the problem it solves right now.

Another effective tactic for lead-generation landing pages is to stress your free offer in the headline and lead.

8. Solve the reader's problem.

Once you hook the reader with emotional copy dramatizing her problem or a powerful free offer, show how your product or your free information can help solve their problem. For example: "Now there is a better, easier, and more effective solution to wobbly restaurant tables that can irritate customers and ruin their dining experience: Table Shox, the world's smallest shock absorber."

To maximize landing page conversion rates, you have to convince the visitor that the quickest route to solving his problem is taking the action indicated on the landing page, and not—as you might be tempted to let him do—surfing your site. That's why I prefer landing pages to appear with no navigation, so the reader's only choice is to respond or not respond; there's no menu of click buttons and hyperlinks to other interesting pages to distract him.

9. Make it timely and current.

The more your online copy ties in with current events and news, the higher your response rates. This is especially critical when selling financial and investment information as well as regulatory compliance products in fields where laws and rules change frequently. Periodically update your landing page copy to reflect current business and economic conditions, challenges, and trends. This shows your visitor that your company is current with and on top of what's happening in your industry today.

10. Stress the money-back guarantee or lack of commitment on the part of the user.

If you allow customers to order products directly from the landing page, make sure you have a money-back guarantee clearly stated on that page. All your competitors give strong money-back guarantees. So you can't get away without doing the same. If your product is good and your copy truthful, your refund rates can be as low as one percent or even less.

If you are generating leads, stress that your offer which might be a white paper, online demonstration, or Webinar—is free. Say there is no obligation to buy and that no salesperson will visit.

CHAPTER 5: MAKE THE BEST OF WHAT YOU'VE GOT

Aside from your company's vital intellectual property and human capital, your most valuable assets are your website and customer database. Marketing automation was initially developed to help companies make the most of those important assets, enabling them to wring every bit of useful data from prospect interaction with their webpages in the hopes that capturing better intelligence would generate more qualified leads. This is a tall order, but plenty of companies have adopted marketing automation solutions that regularly deliver on these goals.

But that's not the whole story. In a cyclical, reiterative progression, marketing automation solutions use prospect data to continually refine the lead generation process, showing you how to build even better webpages, how to optimize your marketing campaigns, and how to get even better prospect data. Better data yields better prospects in greater numbers, which feeds back into a continuously improving lead generation strategy.

This chapter will explain how this cycle of continuous refinement works. It will also outline some of the common mistakes and worst practices that prevent marketers from getting the greatest value from their websites and data.

The company's website.

Conventional wisdom holds that a company's homepage will be the page that visitors land on most frequently. This is an assumption worth examining, but for now it's fair to say that while every company has a homepage, very few actually do a good job of converting traffic from it.

The homepage.

The typical corporate homepage provides dozens of links, some sort of lifestyle image in a banner, and either no call to action or too many calls to action. Lots of digital real estate is occupied by company history, mission statements, and explanations of corporate values. But in the rush to provide as much information and as many options as possible, the traditional homepage frequently alienates visitors, leaving them overwhelmed and possibly confused.

This isn't a book about web design; there are plenty of other resources out there already for that. This guide is for B2B marketers looking for better ways to generate and nurture quality leads for their sales teams. Even so, experience has shown that there are some pretty consistent reasons as to why marketers fail to capitalize on this valuable asset, even allowing their homepage to hinder, rather than help, the sales effort. Some of the most common mistakes marketers make with regard to their corporate website's homepage are outlined below.

1. Too much clutter.

Prospects who have come to your site through search or referral have come there for a specific reason. Odds are that it's not to decide whether to buy stock in the company. Your founding partners were most certainly wonderful people. Your mission statement is probably quite inspiring. But if a prospect has come to your homepage seeking information on a specific product or service that is, if they actually want to buy something from you, they need to see a clear path to achieve this goal immediately upon arriving on your site. Dozens of links, vague jargon- laden copy, and meaningless lifestyle images are not merely confusing they're direct obstacles to that goal. Ideally, your homepage should aim to do no more than provide clear top-level navigation to relevant landing pages with appropriate copy. But if your homepage must do more than this, try to keep it as simple and clean as possible. You want a scannable layout with short paragraphs, bolded subheadings, and bulleted lists. Concentrate on one primary call to action (download a demo, sign up for a webinar, etc.) that encompasses the single key thing that you hope each your site's visitors will do. If you have secondary calls to action, keep them smaller and format them with a different design element, such as a different color or button style.

2. Not segmenting the audience.

The most valuable work that your homepage can do is to allow visitors to quickly self-select the buyer persona that most closely resembles them, as this is where you have the greatest chance for conversion. For example, the audience might be classified by persona into IT person, business analyst, or executive decision-maker. Once you've assigned a persona to a given visitor, marketing automation tools can create a unique profile and serve call-outs that are specific to that persona. Another benefit of persona segmentation is that interior page content and navigation menus can be tailored to the audience, and by tracking these specialized page views, you can capture even more actionable data than you could by just keeping track of general page views. Segmenting your audience from the very first time they reach your homepage will optimize the performance of your marketing automation tools.

3. Not providing contact information.

There's just no excuse for this one. Burying or omitting your contact info, email address, and phone number is just not helpful for lead generation. Every page in your site should have your contact information displayed in a consistent and conspicuous location. Inexplicably, a surprising number of companies omit such details from their homepages. What's worse, this grievous error or omission has become common practice for companies that spend considerable resources driving traffic to their homepage. Don't be shy. Put your contact information out there for all to see. It's the best way to get interested prospects in touch with you.

4. Design flaws that encourage drop-off.

Most site content simply ends at the bottom of the page, leaving the reader to scroll back up to the top, click the back button in the browser, or possibly move on to a different website. Make sure you have a call to action at the bottom of each page, even if it's just a text link to other areas of your site. If you're linking off your site to partner sites or related articles, set the link to open in a new tab or window to avoid losing the visitor.

5. Letting content go stale.

Old content can be a serious embarrassment for your company. The pictures from last year's trade show, featured blog posts that are months old, headlines about expired promotions, and links to last quarter's newsletter or to unused landing pages not only create noise in search engines, but are also a major turn-off for visitors to your site. Ferret out that expired content everywhere on your website, but especially where it appears on your homepage and either properly archive it, or get rid of it altogether.

Your site needs to have consistently fresh content to attract a steady stream of visitors.

6. Wasting precious taglines.

B2B services and products can be quite complex, so it can be hard to summarize a website's purpose in a concise tagline that's short enough for visitors to skim quickly and understand. Unfortunately, the challenge of coming up with a compelling tagline leads many businesses to tag their homepages with meaningless strings of nebulous buzzword-filled expressions, such as leveraging the power of convergence or robust solutions for today's business. These empty word strings say nothing about what your product or service actually is or does, and they do nothing to distinguish your page or company from a world of others. Don't be afraid to say what you do or tell what you sell. If yours is the type of business that would benefit from geographic convenience or a hometown boost, you might also want to consider localizing your homepage tag. At the very least, don't waste the search value of your homepage tag completely. Remember, too, that the page title will be the default entry when users bookmark your site as a Favorite. If you don't want the bookmark to read, "welcome to the home of...", you should alphabetize and tag accordingly.

Landing pages.

The previous section emphasized the importance of a good homepage. But today's web has produced one apparent contradiction: There's really no such thing as a homepage anymore. Search engines have turned this notion of the be-all-end-all homepage on its head because they rank unique webpages, not websites. As Google Analytics guru Avinash Kaushik frequently says, there's no longer any golden door through which all of your visitors will pass. Every page of your website should be looked upon as a point of entry into your website. Every page should have quality content that optimizes prospect conversionopportunities. Give each and every visitor multiple chances to answer your site's calls to action.

In web parlance, any page to which a visitor is directed after clicking an advertisement or an email link is termed a landing page. While the term is relative and might actually be the company's homepage, increasingly these days it's not. A landing page generally displays content that is specific to the advertisement, search keyword, or clicked link. Driving visitors directly to your homepage can be an ineffective method of converting prospects because they are simply presented with too many choices. On the other hand, a landing page offers a streamlined path designed to elicit a specific action by the visitor. Homepages may remain relatively static, but landing pages can be virtual chameleons, constantly changing their content based on specific promotions and seasonal offers, as well as making the improvements that ongoing testing and tracking reveal.

One of the greatest strengths of marketing automation is that it enables the creation of campaign-specific dedicated landing pages without requiring any coding. A WYSIWYG graphical interface allows you to drag and drop elements into the header, content, or footer sections of your landing page and to easily format your page using HTML, rich text, built-in image hosting, and other formatting options to match the look and feel of your brand. These custom landing pages can be easily tested by non-technical users.

Boosting landing page conversion.

For B2B marketers with long and complex sales cycles, conversion typically involves getting a visitor to fill out a form in exchange for something of value: a white paper, a demo, or a free consultation, for example. But there are four distinct groups of people interacting with your landing pages upon whom you're banking for that conversion:

- Visitors who leave within 10 seconds of arriving at your landing page. These make up the vast majority of viewers.

- Visitors who leave when they decide your landing page is not sufficiently compelling. This is the next largest segment.

- Visitors who attempt to fill out your form, but fail or give up and then drop off.

- Visitors who successfully convert to become leads.

As the list suggests, online visitors are busy and easily distracted, so the odds for conversion are usually stacked against you. But there are a number of steps that you can take to boost the effectiveness of your landing pages and to improve those odds significantly. Some of these steps are simple best practices. Others have been made possible by recently developed web technologies. But all of these suggestions will increase the value of your web assets and contribute directly to your online lead generation program.

1. Reinforce the keyword correspondence.

It's all well and good if your target keyword brings a prospect to your page, but you still have to get them to convert. An easy way to start optimizing your landing pages for conversion is to make sure your headlines and images speak directly to the corresponding keywords. If a prospect has clicked on an ad about email marketing, make sure the page they land on is about email marketing and not just a general page with your company logo.

2. Skip the lifestyle shots.

How many times have you gone to a landing page and been greeted with a header graphic that has nothing to do with the offer presented? Do images like a businessman with a laptop or a girl flying a kite really have anything to do with the white paper you are about to re?uest? Probably not. A better approach is to provide a sneak peak of the promised content, such as a small image of the white paper or demo that you're offering. This hero shot gives your visitors something tangible to look forward to and offers a much more compelling reason to convert.

3. Keep it above the fold.

You have tons of great content and fantastic visuals. Save those for your homepage. Your landing page should be a ?uick, clean path to conversion for visitors. Eliminate as much scrolling as possible by keeping most, if not all, of your content above the fold. This axiom was true for newspaper advertising and it is every bit as true for the web.

4. Lay out your value proposition.

Your conversion rate will improve significantly when you're able to answer clearly, and in detail, "what's in it for me?" question that's in the back of all of our minds as we check out new websites. Don't make a guessing game out of your value proposition. If your Buyer's Guide contains (1) a five-page overview, (2) a 100-point checklist of what to look for, (3) a 20-point vendor comparison, and (4) an

ROI calculator, then by all means, say so! Conversions are much more likely when prospects know exactly what they're getting.

5. Brag about your credibility.

Visitors who are not familiar with your company may be hesitant to enter their contact information on your site, even in exchange for something of value. Displaying a few third-party credibility indicators or the seals, certifications, and awards that your company has earned can go a long way in helping to build trust with your visitors. Examples include client feedback and testimonials; site security badges like VeriSign, Thawte, and TRUSTe; ratings from the Better Business Bureau or similar organizations; or any other industry recognitions that your company may have received. Badges such as the Inc. 500 and Marketing Excellence Awards reassure visitors that your company is legitimate and that their information is safe. They also serve as the first step to establishing your brand's reputation with new visitors.

6. Provide assurance of your ethics.

It's always a good idea to include a short privacy statement that ensures prospects that their email address or other information will not be abused or re-sold. It's comforting to see a prominently displayed statement along the lines of, we take our privacy seriously and will never share your contact information. This is a small step, but it can help reassure prospects who may be hesitant to provide their information.

7. Lock up some content.

When a visitor submits a form, many companies simply redirect them to the requested content, be it an article, a white paper, or a demo. A better approach is to clearly set the expectation that you will email a link to the white paper or demo upon form submission. While this does not always guarantee that the lead will give you a valid business email address, it does increase the likelihood. Create this expectation by including a straightforward statement such as Please complete the form below to have the white paper emailed to you.

Using validation on forms allows you to set custom levels of approval to ensure that the email addresses that are entered are not from free providers (often important for B2B marketing), come from a valid email domain, or both. Marketing automation vendors and other quality form hosting providers can actually check the email domain in real-time and display a gentle error message if the validation conditions are not met. When delivering the promised content via email, it's best to send a link to the document's location, rather than sending the document as an attachment. This allows for tracking link click-throughs to determine exactly when the materials were accessed, or if they were even accessed at all. When your sales reps follow up with a phone call, they will benefit much more from knowing when the document was likely read rather than when the email was opened.

Even if you don't have a large library of locked-down content to offer your prospects, providing links to other sections of your website can help you continue tracking your visitors to gain additional insight into their level of interest. Additionally, including links in the email you send your prospects once they've completed a form will provide you with yet another opportunity to reengage those prospects who have already left your site.

8. Give some content away.

Marketing Sherpa cites a case study of a company called INTTRA that took a new approach to forms, a voluntary approach. INTTRA was dealing with a very traditional industry segment with prospects who were more resistant than most with regard to filling out a form in order to view a product demo. Instead of requiring registration, INTTRA decided to allow anyone to view the demo but still provided a form in a sidebar for those who wanted more information.

Despite adopting such an unconventional approach, INTTRA ended up with a surprisingly good conversion rate. Their statistics revealed that 23% of prospects who viewed the demo also filled out the form. Upon converting, these prospects received an autoresponder email that included additional resources, and especially promising leads were passed on to the sales team as appropriate. These leads were obviously qualified since they were actively seeking information. We use a similar technique on our company website. After viewing a free demo that does not require registration, visitors can click a Test Drive button that takes them to a conversion form. This strategy yields a good conversion rate because it makes it so easy for prospects to take the next step towards conversion.

Even though it goes against conventional wisdom, it's still worth considering the notion of having content on your site that isn't locked down behind a form. It can be a good way to ensure that you are capturing the maximum amount of qualified leads and making the process pain-free for your prospects.

9. Get smart about forms.

Forms are your lifeline to your prospects. They're valuable tools that let you collect crucial prospect data so that, once qualified, you can funnel those prospects into the sales pipeline. Typically, prospects visit a website and can only look around so long before they're confronted with that dreaded form asking them to provide more information if they wish to proceed. This is a make-or-break moment in that if the prospect doesn't yet see enough value, he or she won't be persuaded to divulge such details and will abandon the form (and probably your website, too).

Think about the last time this happened to you. You Googled something and clicked on what looked like a promising link, only to encounter a daunting form asking for a whole lot of info after you'd browsed just a few pages on the site. Either the form was too long and tedious to bother filling out, or it asked you for far more information than you were comfortable providing.

Why is it asking for my mother's maiden name? you asked incredulously, promptly clicking back to try a different search result. You made a quick cost-benefit calculation that the tradeoff (your mother's maiden name in exchange for a view of the page you wanted to see) wasn't worth it, and you abandoned the form and navigated away from that site, possibly forever.

You obviously don't want the same outcome with visitors to your own site. You want them to come in and have a look around, be dazzled by what you have to offer, and gladly give up a few bits of personal data in exchange for the multitude of benefits your site so clearly provides. Make sure you don't lose them at this critical juncture!

Remember that, just like you, your prospects are also prone to form abandonment. But you can help them work through their abandonment issues by designing simple, un-intimidating forms that they don't mind filling out.

Here are some best practices for reducing form abandonment:

1. Don't waste your visitor's time.

Don't make your visitors repeat themselves in the same form, and don't ask them for the same piece of information more than once. Whenever possible, use time savers like drop-downs and checkboxes that don't require prospects to craft their own response (more on this below). This approach also makes it much easier for you to aggregate data and automate processes on the back end.

2. Minimize the required fields.

Nothing is more frustrating for most visitors than arriving on a landing page and seeing a massive form with most or all of its fields marked with the —required field‖ red asterisk of death. Companies that ask visitors to fill in more than a handful of fields in the first interaction are just encouraging drop-off. B2B sales cycles by their very nature are often multi-touch and complex, and each touchpoint provides another opportunity to collect data, which means that marketers have more time to compile prospect profiles. Why risk alienating prospects by rushing to get everything up front?

3. Use progressive profiling.

Using conditional fields allows you to progressively build an in-depth prospect profile by asking for just one or two data points during each prospect interaction, depending on the information they've already provided.

Picture this: A visitor hits your landing page and is asked for her name, email address, and company in exchange for a white paper. Twenty minutes later, she requests a flash demo and is asked for her job title. In three weeks, she returns to your site and is asked for her department in exchange for a case study. A few days later, she is asked about her buying stage after requesting a live demonstration. This is an unintrusive and non-threatening way to collect crucial data, bit by bit, until you have a complete representation of this prospect and her buying intentions.

The same form is used for all the content across your site, but progressive profiling allows the form to intelligently display only the fields you're missing for that particular prospect. Marketing automation tools employ cookies to identify returning prospects and remember what information these prospects have already provided. Forms with progressive profiling features allow you to set up tiers in advance so that each time a prospect returns, they will be asked the appropriate questions. Try to keep the first form down to four fields at the most, and guide prospects to view other compelling content across your site in order to gradually obtain additional data from them.

4. Tone down your error messages.

In terms of the top website visitor annoyances, harsh in-your-face error messages come a close second to lengthy forms. Imagine that your visitor has taken the time to fill out and submit a form in order to receive your white paper. Instead of the satisfying Thank you message she expects to pop up, she's greeted with a glaring red error message or worse, an empty form that forces her to start all over again. Guess what? Chances are, she won't bother.

The quick fix for this common issue is to handle error validation instantly. Your forms should be configured to display an error message as soon as a visitor fails to correctly complete the required field. For example, if a visitor is filling out a form and enters an invalid state abbreviation, make sure that your form immediately displays a corresponding prompt: "Please enter a valid state." This warning is immediate but much more subtle, and it's preferable in that it allows your visitor to correct entries without losing the data they've already provided, reducing the risk of form abandonment.

5. Test, test, and test again.

The one great truth about landing pages is that you can always improve upon them with testing. Marketing automation platforms usually allow you to set up a simple multivariate test, which automatically distributes your incoming traffic to two separate landing pages. The landing pages should be very similar, perhaps varying only very slightly in design, copy, or content. Eventually you'll be able to evaluate which variation has a higher conversion rate, which will help you develop the most effective landing page possible. But don't stop here. You should continually test and refine landing pages because there's always room for improvement, especially when you have good data.

At a loss as to which landing page attributes you should be testing? Try experimenting with a few of the following variables:

•Headline; Keep it short and compelling; the headline should always convey an immediate benefit to the reader.

•Offer; Experiment with offering a variety of incentives (white papers, free consultations, demos, and other motivating content) to find out what prospects view as most valuable.

•Visuals; Try using compelling, sneak peek, shots of your white paper cover, an internal page, or a demo screenshot to stimulate additional interest in your offerings.

•Form length; If you started with a lengthy form, try removing a few required fields and see if your conversion rate improves.

•Form fields; Try substituting fields (e.g., department vs. job title) or changing up formatting by adding more user-friendly features like drop-down menus and checkboxes.

Although testing can be difficult and tedious to carry out manually, marketing automation solutions can make complex tests a breeze by automatically assigning traffic to each of your page designs and reporting on the results.

Whatever your need for forms may be, marketing automation solutions simplify the form-building process through an intuitive drag-and-drop interface. Because forms are so easy to create, they become an organic and flexible source for getting clean, accurate, relevant prospect data which is what you really want from the investment you've made in your company's website and landing pages.

Getting Value From Your Data

If you're considering a marketing automation solution for inbound lead generation, you are probably most excited about the vast quantity of data you can collect on prospects and their needs. But you can also greatly enhance the quality of this data by utilizing your marketing automation platform as a data cleaner. And there's plenty of incentive for keeping that data clean. According to B2B marketing strategist Ardath Albee, the revenue lift that will result from merely cleaning up dirty prospect data can be as great as 70%.

Keeping It Clean

While CRM systems perform many functions effectively, deduplication of prospect data does not seem to be one of them. To keep your CRM data, clean in terms of the leads that come from your website, take these important steps:

1.Automatically check for duplicates in existing data.

Prospects can enter your CRM through many different ways—through filling out forms, dropping by your booth at trade shows, subscribing to newsletters, and so on. Most companies don't check their CRM to see if the prospect is already there. But the same person filling out several forms, or completing one form multiple times, can create unwanted noise in our database. Funneling all of your leads through a marketing automation platform before they enter your CRM will match records based on criteria like email address in order to distinguish new records from duplicates.

2.Get data validation at the form level.

At a minimum, you should ensure that email addresses are in a valid format (blank@site.com) before letting them enter your database. An even better approach is setting up your form to ping the domain in real time to ensure that it has an actual mail exchange record. This latter method prevents prospects from entering an invalid address such as abcdef@abcdef.com, which would pass the first test. You could take this one step further by actually refusing to accept addresses from free email providers. Generally speaking, you don't want sales reps to waste time following up with prospects that supplied Yahoo!, Hotmail, or Gmail addresses.

For a visitor whose email address fails validation, be sure to provide a soft error message as soon as they tab off the field, as opposed to having them click the submit button, only to be surprised by a glaring error notification. This simple step will discourage drop-off among legitimate prospects while still weeding out unsuitable leads from your screening process.

3.Limit choices via drop-downs instead of free-form text.

Using drop-down lists or menus and other structured data fields like checkboxes is a great way to standardize your data while streamlining the visitor experience. This practice makes prospect data fields like industry and job title much more usable later, as it helps you avoid permutations of the same title (e.g., VP, Vice President, etc.). Predefined field values result in better, cleaner data for you. And because forms can be filled out much faster than with free text fields, they waste less visitor time, contributing to the likelihood that your prospects will offer up what is asked of them.

Keep bots away with built-in spam prevention. If left unchecked, bots can quickly fill a company's database with gibberish. Many companies (including Google) stop bots in their tracks by using captchas, an additional field where you enter a string of text or a number to prove that you are indeed a human. Captchas, while effective in term of spam prevention, can frustrate visitors and drive down your conversion rate, so you may want to consider using a hidden spam trap that humans will never need to see or deal with.

Each of these techniques can be accomplished either through custom programming or via a good marketing automation solution. Either way, the technology is out there, and taking these precautions will make your life easier by keeping your data cleaner.

Activity Tracking

While 99% of web analytics programs collect information at the macro level, the analytics tools built into marketing automation solutions track traffic at the individual or micro level. Advanced prospect activity tracking allows you to view a log of every touchpoint with your prospect. You can see the pages your prospect has visited, find out which files they've downloaded, keep track of email correspondence, and more. Additionally, tracking tools record all activities that occurred prior to the prospect's conversion. With this information, you can nurture leads much more efficiently and help your sales team close more deals. As prospects interact with your website, their scores will increase, promoting the most active prospects to the top of the follow-up list.

Track Anonymous Visitors.

Although most B2B marketers would love to follow up with all of the visitors to your website, the majority of traffic will unfortunately be anonymous. Some studies have shown that as few as 2% of website visitors actually become viable prospects. Wouldn't it be helpful if you could somehow track the other 98% of these visitors? Marketing automation can help you do that, too.

A good marketing automation solution can record abandoned or updated data from a form that wasn't submitted. Suppose that your anonymous visitor tracking shows that a prospect entered three different email addresses before successfully completing the form. He first entered a Yahoo! address and was prompted to use a non-free address. He then tried to give a made-up address and was prompted to give a valid email. He finally broke down and entered his corporate email address. This sort of scenario might indicate that this prospect is wary of being contacted via email. It might be more appropriate to put leads like this on a nurturing track rather than contacting them immediately with a sales pitch.

Tracking your website's visitors, even the anonymous ones, can tell you much more than you might think. Being able to track at the individual prospect level is like playing detective with anonymous visitors to your website and can greatly improve your use of marketing automation. Here's what you can learn with the click of a mouse:

- IP address.

Some marketing automation solutions can use a visitor's IP address to find out what company or organization is visiting your site. Often the IP address doesn't provide much value, as it comes from a generic internet service provider (ISP). But a small percentage, (usually 0.5–10%) of IP addresses can be identified at the company level; these are primarily mid-size and large companies (hospitals, government entities, and institutions of higher education) that have their own connectivity (T1 or T3 line). Marketing automation tools can easily identify visitors from such companies, and once you know this, you can have your sales team act on that information accordingly.

- Browser and OS.

People who use Firefox are typically more tech-savvy than those who use Internet Explorer. Mac and Linux users are a distinguished category for companies selling technology products or services.

- Hostname/Referrer.

The most informative field within this feature is the Hostname/Referrer, which tells you the origin of a visitor, including their IP address and the name under which it's registered. From a marketing standpoint, tracking patterns of anonymous visitors can help you identify trends in particular industry verticals and potential new audiences for your product or service. From a sales perspective, this information has several uses. If you're in the middle of the sales cycle, knowing that there have been numerous visits originating from a company that's evaluating your product gives a good indication as to just how serious they are. This information can also be useful in helping salespeople locate appropriate contacts at a prospective client company.

- Search origination.

Knowing which search engine (Yahoo, Google, Bing, etc.) brought a particular visitor to your site can help you determine where your best leads are coming from and in what proportions, thereby improving allocation of your marketing spend.

- Page views and interaction time.

Analyzing page views and interaction time metrics allow you to see exactly which components of your site each individual prospect has been browsing and for how long. This tells you what things are most (and least) important to potential customers, allowing you to customize your lead nurturing strategy and tailor your sales pitch accordingly. Page views and interaction time can also be good indicators of whether or not your page design is meeting your expectations for providing useful, coherent content to a particular market segment or prospect persona.

•Search term.

The nature of a search—that is, which search terms brought the searcher to your site—can tell you a great deal about how serious a particular visitor might be. If a visitor searches for the answer to a very general question, what is marketing automation, they may or may not be worth pursuing. If they're searching for your product by name, however, you can bet that they're interested in your product and didn't just happen upon your site by chance. Knowing the specific search phrases people use to find your site can provide a wealth of information that quantitative examinations of conversion rates just can't convey. This knowledge also enables you to better optimize your pages based on popular keywords for determining which campaigns are most effective.

With Great Power Comes Great Responsibility

The information gleaned from the advanced tracking features built into most marketing automation solutions can put you in a powerful position—one you can use to great advantage during the sales process. But it's important to use this information wisely. Though most people are aware of the ability to track activities online, some might still be averse to the idea of being tracked themselves. The first time you call a prospect within a few minutes of their visiting your website, they may brush it off as a coincidence. If you call them within a few minutes of every single visit, they might start to feel a little bit intimidated. It's crucial to make sure that you and your sales team are on the same page about how much immediate follow-up is too much.

The one exception to this guideline is when someone requests immediate follow-up, as with a support form or a contact form. In these cases, a fast response time would be interpreted positively. Marketing automation tools can give you a jump-start by sending you alerts; some platforms even incorporate web-to-phone technology that instantly connects sales and services representatives to incoming prospects by phone as soon as a request is submitted. As a general rule, simply keep in mind that when calling on prospects you should use your insider knowledge to wow them with a personalized pitch, not to scare them by coming on too strong.

Winning The SEO Arms Race.

Search engine optimization (SEO) has become the arms race of the internet age. Getting high placement in search results through the best page rankings is the prize that's perpetually just beyond reach, and companies will do almost anything to achieve victory. Competition to be the winner, has spawned an entire industry of SEO consultants for hire. Organizations that have become reasonably successful at optimization follow best practices for on-page SEO, have great internal linking structure, and run inbound linking campaigns. At the end of the day, however, what often separates good rankings from great rankings is the sheer amount of useful content that your organization can generate on a regular basis.

Right now you're probably thinking, Here we go again. Another lecture on the need for regularly updated quality content. Unfortunately, if you want to be competitive, you're right. Today's B2B marketers are an overtaxed bunch. They're often asked to do more now with fewer resources than they might have enjoyed a few years ago. But fortunately, if your organization is a products company, you probably already have a wealth of content that could be helping your current search rankings.

Most companies keep their knowledge bases, customer communities, and forums under lock and key, afraid that competitors or prospects may see their warts or proprietary information. The reality is that your documentation and community sites likely contain a tremendous amount of content that can and should be indexable by search engines. Assuming your documentation is complete and your community is well taken care of, you have nothing to hide. Competitors probably already know more about you than you can imagine, and prospects will likely be encouraged by the transparency and happy to have access to your community during the buying process.

Any time one of your support reps answers a question via email but does not have relevant documentation to link to, he or she should write up an answer, post it to the site, and send the URL to the client. Of course, it helps if you have a simple content management system, a community management system, or a user forum so that your reps can adopt this standardized process with zero IT involvement. This allows your support team and also your user community to become content creators for you. You'll find that the number of pages indexed on your documentation or community site quickly outstrips your corporate site and that you start to rank well for many long tail keywords. Who wouldn't want to double or triple their number of quality pages in Google or Bing's indexes?

What can you start making available to the search engines? Consider creating and promoting easily accessible content such as product documentation, FAQs, blogs, community forums, and idea exchanges. And who says that a support ticket can't be an opportunity for SEO-boosting content? Think outside the box to come out ahead in the great SEO race.

CHAPTER 6: WHAT EXACTLY IS B2B MARKETING?

When you hear "marketing", what do you think of? Most people think of consumer marketing (Business to Consumer or B2C).

Unfortunately, people's familiarity with B2C marketing leads to confusion and frustration with B2B marketing. While there are important consistencies between the two, there are significant differences.

B2B marketing is less about show (grabbing the buyer's attention in whatever way works) and more about tell (why is your product or service better than a competitor's?). It is vital for B2B companies to establish credibility in the eyes of target buyers. This is because B2B decisions generally carry more risk than B2C decisions. For example, if I buy a new laptop and it doesn't meet my needs, I (and I alone) bear the consequences of that decision. If I make a similar decision when buying laptops for my workplace, my colleagues and I both have to live with the consequences. And if that decision is extremely bad, not only will my colleagues be upset, but my job may be at risk or my business may suffer.

There are four components to B2B marketing.

1. Defining where and how the company will compete: This entails the research and decisions that define the company's focus related to the markets the company participates in and its position in those markets (market intelligence and market strategy).

2. Generating awareness and leads: These are the activities that sit at the top of the sales funnel. These are

often called "lead generation" or "awareness activities", as they bring in the leads that the business development team works to convert to revenues (lead generation and education).

3. Supporting the sales process: These are the activities that sit alongside the funnel and produce a positive perception of the company, as well as tangible tools and information that support the sales process (branding and sales support).

4. Creating loyal customers: These are the activities that sit at the end of the funnel and ensure that existing customers stay loyal to the company and buy again, and in greater quantities, in the future.

Here are some of the factors that make B2B and B2C marketing different:

One of the most common questions you will hear from CEOs of small and mid-size B2B companies is, "Marketing hasn't been a priority for us because of the resources required—so where do we even start?"

Their question reveals the challenges of B2B marketing. Many CEOs understand that marketing is important for their businesses, but they haven't been able to tackle it effectively. They know they should be doing it better, and they want to do it better, but they don't know how. That's understandable, because there are some significant challenges for B2B companies when it comes to marketing.

The main challenge is a resource gap. For B2B companies, marketing is rarely a core competence. In small and mid-size B2B companies, marketing is typically a small function that doesn't warrant its own executive or team. So the Head of Marketing is often someone who has another job—the CEO, the COO, or the VP of Business Development. The problem is that these executives have other priorities. If there is a problem in the plant, the COO isn't going to stop to write a press release. If there is a new sales opportunity, the VP of Sales isn't going to film a video case study. Because their other responsibilities are prioritized, marketing activities are put on hold whenever the executive is pulled away to another area, which happens frequently.

Because of the nature of marketing, this leads to poor results. Marketing is a business function that demands consistency. It's like dating—a slow and steady approach is far more effective than a courtship that blows hot and cold unpredictably. Unfortunately, many B2B companies deal with marketing in a reactive way. They ignore it until there is an issue: a trade show that's a few weeks away and hasn't been planned for, or an article that needs to be submitted to an industry journal the next morning. This leads to a huge amount of wasted marketing investment, not to mention stress, frustration, and poor representation of the company.

The other gap is one of expertise. Very few non-marketing executives have B2B marketing expertise. Heck, relatively few marketers have B2B marketing expertise. While there are many training grounds for B2C marketing, there are few for B2B marketing. A junior marketer within a B2B company might know about customers, buying behaviour, and industry trends, but they rarely know how to put a strategic B2B marketing plan together or how to manage the multiple moving parts it entails. There are many elements to a comprehensive marketing plan—from graphic design, to search engine optimization, to event planning, and beyond. It's challenging and rare for one person to be skilled at everything.

B2B companies are often technical in nature, and sometimes struggle to communicate the value of their products and services clearly and effectively. They are founded by someone who has technical knowledge of the service or product that the company provides. These founders are exceptionally competent in their area of expertise, and they are also pretty good salespeople—they are successful in connecting with the target market and selling their offering (or else they wouldn't still be around as a company). But marketing is not their comfort zone and they don't like the notion of promoting what they do. They often believe that if they make a product that is very, very good, customers will figure that out and come running to buy it. Sadly, that just doesn't happen.

Turnover of marketing staff is another issue for B2B companies. It is difficult to retain marketing personnel in smaller companies because of the lack of mentorship, opportunities for promotion, and the chance to constantly develop their skills. As a result, turnover of marketing personnel is high in B2B companies, which leads to gaps between marketing initiatives and too much time spent training new people.

And finally, there is confusion around tactics. It's common for one type of marketing to become the 'flavor of the month' (e.g. social media, search engine optimization, videos). Someone in a company will get excited about the potential of a tactic and will invest time or money in it. The trouble is that no single B2B marketing tactic can deliver maximum results. Making a video doesn't do anything unless the video is effectively promoted and shared with prospects. Improving search engine optimization won't help land new business if your website doesn't enable prospects to take the next step in learning more about the company. It's dangerous for B2B companies to jump on a tactic without integrating it into a cohesive marketing plan and considering if it's the right tactic for the company. For example, social media may be a hot topic, but if your industry is barely online, does it make sense for your company? You'd be surprised how many marketers fail to ask this question before "going social".

Despite these challenges, there is every reason for B2B companies to put marketing to work for them. Effective marketing builds awareness and a positive perception of the company, generates leads, and helps grow revenue. B2B companies that effectively use marketing work less to get leads and secure new business. They travel less and maintain full pricing more often. Marketing enables them to make the leap from a relatively successful company to a tremendously successful one.

So let's talk about B2B marketing strategy.

CHAPTER 7:

HOW TO DEVELOP A SOLID B2B MARKETING STRATEGY

A marketing strategy will save a company tens or hundreds of thousands of dollars by avoiding marketing activities that do not deliver the results they seek and by focusing resources in the highest value areas.

Good B2B marketing involves a roadmap. This is especially important for small and mid-size companies that have limited resources. Defining a strategy helps a company clarify its focus. What market or markets are you going after, which markets and marketing opportunities will you say no to? There are thousands of ways to spend marketing dollars. The challenge is to figure out which ways will be most effective. Most companies don't have any mechanisms for turning down marketing opportunities, so they make decisions about marketing that are ad-hoc and based on the sentiment of the decision maker in a particular moment. Companies need a strategy to focus their efforts and hold their marketing accountable for defined results.

Business schools usually teach marketing strategy as "the four Ps"—product, price, place, and promotion. In my experience, the four Ps isn't a very practical definition. The reality is that most companies are fixed in their product and place (what they make and how they sell it). They can't switch from making airplane components to making farm equipment. Yes, they can introduce new products and services, but they won't make major switches. Likewise, a shift from selling through distributors to having a direct sales force is unlikely—it can happen, but it doesn't happen often.

Because of that reality, I use a different approach to defining B2B marketing strategy. I believe there are three areas that companies need to define:

- **Target Market**: Who are the ideal customers, what needs and priorities do they have, how do they make purchase decisions, and how do they learn?

- **Value Proposition**: Why should buyers buy from you? What unique factors does your company have that are important to customers? The more specific, objective, and quantified you can be, the better. This is also known as "competitive advantage".

- **Messaging**: This is tied to value proposition. What specific messages will you use to attract the attention of prospective buyers to convey that you understand their needs and have a solution for them?

To get answers to these questions, I use a basic framework called "the three Cs". The Cs stand for Company, Customers, and Competition. Good marketing strategy lies at the intersection of these three Cs.

The three C's allow you to put together an effective marketing strategy quickly and clearly. It leverages the expertise that is resident in your organization and includes external research to validate and augment what is already known. There are three steps in the process:

- Step 1 is an internal process to gather information available within the company. It includes a company workshop and interviews with staff and management. It also collects available reports on sales, profitability, and marketing.

- Step 2 is external—it includes research and interviews with customers, industry experts, and competitors to augment internal information and validate, or disprove, the hypotheses you've made in Step One.

• Step 3 brings together the data and insight you've gained on the three C's to confirm the marketing strategy—target market, value proposition, and messaging.

The first step in developing a solid marketing strategy is to confirm information about your company. What are your goals? Where are you relative to those goals? What do you offer? How do you make money? This chapter walks you through a practical, step-by-step process for obtaining this information.

There are five questions to answer in the company assessment. Most of them are straightforward and can be accomplished through a team workshop or individual meetings with the managers and staff. Some answers will come from reports that already exist within the company.

Part One: Company Goals

What are your company's goals? The direction you want your company to go has a big impact on what type of marketing you should engage in. Below is a list of possible business goals. Which ones apply to your company? Keep in mind these are overall business goals, not marketing goals.

If your goals aren't on this list, don't worry—just add them.

• To become the dominant player in the market

• To position the company for strategic acquisition

• To become highly profitable with stable revenues

- To maintain market leadership
- To expand into new geographies
- To expand into new industries
- To establish channel partnerships
- To acquire a certain number of new customers

It's dangerous to select more than three or four of these goals. Prioritizing will help you focus and identify where limited resources can be invested. It can also help reveal what types and amount of marketing make sense given what you want to achieve with the business.

Part Two: Products and Offerings

Clearly defining the features and benefits that you deliver to customers is essential in developing powerful marketing. Hopefully you have a strong sense of what you provide to the market, but this process crystallizes what is different and special about each of your offerings. It will help you identify the most powerful value you provide, to whom you provide it, and the potential messages that will resonate with them.

You can do this by using a simple matrix. List your products and services across the top and then customers, technical features, and benefits down the side.

Work with your team to identify all the features and benefits you provide to the different types of customers you can and do serve. Be specific, objective, and quantified. For example, stating that you provide great customer service doesn't say anything meaningful to prospects, because everyone says that. Instead, specify what it is about your customer service that makes it so great. Do you guarantee that you'll have a technician available within a business day? Do you return all calls within an hour? Does your product allow customers to reduce their energy consumption by 20%? The more specific, objective, and quantified you can be, the more powerful your marketing.

Part Three: Revenues and Profit Performance

This process helps identify areas of success. It's a straight-forward exercise that pinpoints where you make your profits. It will help clarify where you want to dedicate marketing efforts and where you may not want to dedicate any effort at all.

Consider these questions:

- What is your total revenue / profit for the past 3 years?
- What is your revenue / profit by product?
- What is your revenue / profit by customer type?

The answers will reveal where your company is most successful. Every company makes investments that are expected to turn into profits in the long term. Is your company making profits where it expects to? If not, you may want to reconsider where you allocate resources, including marketing resources.

Part Four: Opportunities and Threats

Conduct internal interviews with your staff to obtain insights into perceived opportunities and threats. I'm always impressed by the depth and breadth of insight that can come from sales people, technicians, and customer service reps. Anyone who deals directly with customers has a very powerful perspective on how customers think and what they really want from your company. They often have ideas for new products or services and thoughts about emerging threats. Sitting down with these team members and having a structured conversation will allow you to capture these perspectives.

Part Five: Marketing Audit

The last step in the company assessment is to audit your marketing activities and assets. What marketing tactics do you undertake and how do they perform? How many leads does each activity generate? What tools do you have in your marketing toolkit? What collateral (brochures, tech spec sheets, project portfolios, case studies, white papers, etc) do you have? How do they represent your brand? Do they communicate your value proposition? Are they consistent?

Make sure to include these areas in your assessment:

• Website and analytics—Google Analytics, and consider using a tool like Hubspot or gShiftLabs for benchmarking data

• eNewsletters—your email provider (e.g. Constant Contact, Mail Chimp) will provide you with benchmarking data on open rates and click throughs

• Printed material—company overviews, solution overviews, and any other printed materials

• Thought leadership—articles, case studies, white papers, ebooks, videos

• Events—trade shows, webinars, and lunch and learns

• CRM system—review existing system (or lack thereof)

Compile your findings

By gathering answers to these five questions, you can establish a strong foundation. Where is the company now, what are its strengths, its assets, its opportunities? Where has it performed well in the past? Where might its opportunities lie in the future? How is the marketing function performing?

Once you've completed the assessment, take one sheet of paper and summarize your findings. This sounds easy but is often quite difficult. It can take a few rounds of work. Start by writing your key findings from each question on a page. Then work to distill the five pages down to one page of key findings. Walk away from your review for a few days and come back to it—did you miss anything important, have you included anything that isn't really essential?

Once you have the key findings, identify the implications of those findings. What do the facts mean for your business? How do you need to react to capitalize on opportunities and neutralize threats? Should you focus on a particular product line? Customer type? Is there anything you're doing that should be stopped?

And finally, store all the information you have gathered in one place—after all this effort, you should capture the information and make it easy for your team to access in future.

Understanding what customers need and how they buy.

The next component of the three C's model is customers. For the companies I've worked with, this step provided a tremendous amount of value. It's amazing that assessing customers and their needs could be a novel concept. But for many companies it is. The clients that Mezzanine serves are often thrilled that we will be interviewing their customers and prospects to systematically identify why and how they buy, what emerging needs they have, and what perceptions they have of the company and the competition.

The purpose of the customer assessment is to intimately understand buying behaviour. There are two ways to gather this knowledge—secondary and primary research. Secondary research relies on published information (such as industry reports) and capturing the customer knowledge that already exists in your company (sales, customer service, and management). Primary research involves conducting interviews and creating surveys directed at current or prospective customers.

Secondary Research

Secondary research is good if you need some high-level data, like the size and structure of particular industries you're considering to enter. It can help you make decisions about which industries to pursue or potential untapped markets or customer bases.

The challenge with secondary research is that there's either too much or too little. There are vast amounts of information

on some industries and markets, and next to none on others—particularly at the level of depth you'll need in order to get a solid understanding of customers.

Because of this, I usually start the customer assessment process by searching online to see what's available—published reports can be useful as a starting point for areas you're not familiar with (e.g. a new geography or sector)—but be prepared to also do research on your own.

Also consider using your networks on social media such as Twitter, LinkedIn Groups, Google+, or Facebook to identify secondary data and reports that can be useful to you.

Primary Research

Primary research is at the heart of successful marketing strategy. It provides the necessary depth of insight. There are five steps to getting valuable customer insight.

Step One—What do you need to know?

Identify what information you want. Put a guideline together to structure your discussions with customers, prospects, and others. It will ensure you collect and capture all the great information you're about to hear. Here are the basic areas to investigate:

Buyer Characteristics: What industry are they in? What kind of organization? What is their role (job title)? How long have they been in that role? What are their responsibilities?

Decision-Making Process: Who's involved in making the purchase decision? Who has the power to say yes or no? When was the last purchase of this kind made? How was it made and why was a certain vendor chosen

Decision Criteria: What are the buyer's priorities? What formal or informal criteria do they have for evaluating the purchase? Is there a strict structure to the criteria or a loose framework? Are there set budgets in place?

Timeline: Are purchases made on a regular basis? At what point in the business cycle does demand exist? How long is the purchase process?

Learning and Influences: How do they keep up with the industry? What trade publications do they read, what industry associations do they belong to, what trade shows do they go to? Do they attend lunch and learns? Webinars? Do they read white papers? E-newsletters?

Step Two—Start with what you already know

You can complete this step at the same time as the workshop for the company assessment.

There is a tremendous amount of customer knowledge within your own company. In a workshop or individual interviews ask the sales team, customer service representatives, and management what they know or suspect. Get answers to the questions you identified in Step One. Not everyone will know everything, and they may be uncertain about particular topics, but usually a good portion of what you need to know is already resident in your company.

One caveat—your team will know a lot about your existing customers but much less about non-customers. They may also know how your customers interact with your company but not how they interact with competitors or with each other. Don't assume that what you learn from your internal sources is the full story. You will still need to do research directly among customers and non-customers to develop a marketing strategy that can help you grow your business both within and beyond your existing customer base.

Step Three—Conduct research

There are several methods you can use to gain and validate information on customers and prospects:

- In-person, One-on-One Interviews are a great way to gather in-depth insights, pain points, and issues in particular industries. In person interviews are a great way to build rapport and assess context of the answers beyond the words, such as through body language. However, this requires a substantial amount of time to properly execute and, depending on your resources and the location of your customers, this may not be a realistic option.

- Telephone Interviews are cost effective and avoid geographical constraints. The key with telephone interviews is the quality of the interviewee. Though you can easily speak to large volumes of people, you are better to speak with fewer, expert interviewees to gain deeper, more useful insights.

- Focus Groups can offer powerful insights. However, logistics can make them difficult. One way to do focus groups efficiently is to convene them around an industry conference. If everyone is going to be in the same city for a major industry event, you can often get people together for a two-hour session. You may need to offer them an incentive. You may hear different things in a group than you would one-on-one, because group-think can be a problem if your focus group isn't moderated properly.

- Surveys can be quick and easy, especially through online survey tools. However, the response rates are often low, which limits their value. You also must be cautious that the respondents are the people that you want to hear from. Another challenge is that many companies are not experts at developing effective survey questions, so you can end up with results that actually hurt your understanding of customer needs rather than enhance it.

Consider a third-party research company for customer and prospect research. Customers will be more truthful about your performance if they're speaking to someone outside of the company and can be confident that confidentiality will be kept.

Include satisfied customers as well as former customers in your process. And don't forget prospects—those people and companies who have never bought from you. Hearing what they know, or don't know, about your company is extremely useful. Include a spectrum of potential buyers across industries and functions to get the best possible range of perspectives.

How many interviews do you need? I find that six to eight interviews per B2B segment is sufficient in developing an understanding of the group. The challenge, of course, is that you don't know the segments before you do the interviews! But in general, twelve to thirty interviews will allow you to identify the segments and understand the differences in buying behaviour between them. The larger or more diverse your set of buyers, the more interviews you'll want to do.

Step Four—Analyze the data

It's easy to conduct primary research and then think you're done. But the raw data doesn't do much for you. It's the analysis that delivers the useful insight needed for your marketing plan. Here are some tips to help you make the most of your research:

1. Develop hypotheses (using the internal perspectives) and use the interviews or surveys to confirm or refute the hypotheses.

2. Look for connections and patterns in the information. It's ok to use your gut to spot trends or ignore outliers, but you also need to look at the data systematically to ensure you aren't creating biases.

3. Assess what people did say as well as what they didn't.

4. Summarize key data points, notable findings, and answers to your original questions. Create charts, tables, and graphs to organize and display your findings—this is important if you are sharing your research with others.

Step Five—Identify segments

The last step is to identify the different segments that exist in the market. This is important, because it's rare that a company can serve all segments. Different segments have different needs, so it makes sense that they look to different suppliers. Defining the segments by needs will help you identify which segments you will target—and which you won't.

Segments differ based on buying characteristics. For example, if Buyer A is price insensitive, relies on consulting engineers to inform her decisions, and buys for offshore rigs, they are in a different segment than Buyer B who is primarily budget driven and buying for a small, commercial office.

Compile your findings

As you did at the end of the company analysis process, the last step in the Customer process is to compile your results and identify your key findings.

The final C is understanding the competitive landscape.

Competitive intelligence is tricky. It's hard for companies to know how much they should obtain, and it's even harder to actually obtain it. In my experience, larger companies are likely to dedicate resources to competitive intelligence (CI). Smaller companies like the idea but usually don't have the resources to commit to it. They argue that what the competition does is irrelevant, because the company is pursuing a particular direction and doesn't need to respond directly to competitors. Others believe they are small enough that they need to focus on their clients alone, not the competition.

These arguments don't hold up, because the point of CI isn't to copy the competition but rather to know what the competition is doing so that you can do something different that aligns with market needs and your company's strengths. A company needs to know what the competition is doing to maintain a sustainable, competitive advantage.

What information about competitors should you gather?

Basic CI includes identifying who the competition is (both direct and indirect competitors) and obtaining an overview of their characteristics: product lines, distribution, pricing, reputation, market share, business development process and team, and any other parameters you identify as crucial. You may not need to gather all of this information—select the topics that are most relevant for the competition you face and the marketing decisions you need to make.

Use a matrix to give your competitive intelligence process structure. List the competitors you're assessing along the top and the parameters along the side. When gathering information, do not use arbitrary ratings, get actual data and include it. It's important to complete the matrix in its entirety—consistency in your understanding of the competition is important so you can confidently use the information to build your strategy.

Gathering Information the right way

CI can sound like a sexy undertaking but don't turn it into a dumpster diving affair. There are reasonable and unreasonable ways to do CI. The latter can land companies in the headlines and are more likely to hurt than help.

In most cases, a third party is needed to obtain competitive intelligence. They can get access to details and people that you cannot simply by merit of being independent. This method requires the most financial commitment, but often it is the only viable solution for getting useful CI.

The simplest starting point for CI (although it's just the starting point, not the be-all and end-all) is online. Looking at a competitor's website can provide a baseline of information, including marketing collateral (brochures, press releases, etc.). These can be revealing—are competitors expanding into a new region? Opening a new distribution centre? Launching a new product?

 However, be wary of what you find onlin. Many companies, especially smaller and mid-size, don't keep their sites up to date, and how they look online may be entirely different from reality.

Check for posted job opportunities. Learning about the type of people your competition is hiring can give you clues to what market niches they are exploring, which divisions they are expanding, and what product or service lines they are prioritizing. Social media such as LinkedIn can be a great resource to understand who's moving into (or out of) a competitor.

Ask your business development team. Their direct contact with customers provides them access to strong market knowledge. Leverage their relationships with customers to assess the competition. Ask for their objective opinions.

Look for former employees on LinkedIn. As long as they are not under confidentiality agreements, they may be able to share some insight.

Consider talking with head-hunters, industry association personnel, or other industry watchers who may have views on the industry. You'll be amazed by what people will tell you, if only you ask.

Mystery shopping will sometimes work for B2B companies. Buy something from your key competitors to understand every facet of their customer experience. Are they responsive? What is their sales process? Do they provide follow up after the sale? Although this method allows you to gather data via personal, first-hand experience, it is quite tricky, because it isn't always possible to buy something from your competition and when you can, it will involve an investment.

Most importantly—ask customers. They almost always have useful knowledge of your competition and are often willing to share.

Finally, don't make the mistake of using your competitive intelligence in a reactive way. If your company's competitive advantage lies in a unique product or service quality, don't alter your core strategy just because your competitor is altering theirs. Focus on your own strengths and customer needs.

Once you have completed the competitive intelligence, do the same analysis as the one you did at the culmination of the company and customer steps. What are the key findings, what are the strengths and weaknesses of competitors, what direction are they heading in, and what might it mean for your company?

Defining your marketing strategy

Now that you have gathered a full view of your company, customers, and competition, you can develop the marketing strategy.

Start by summarizing the results of the three C's. In each section, you created a few pages of key findings and implications. Put all of these together and evaluate them as a whole. What do can you take away from them? Did you learn from the company analysis that your organization has the largest market share, and one segment of your customers values buying from a stable supplier? If so, perhaps one of your main marketing messages should be that your company is the largest supplier of your product or service and, as a result, you provide stability and economies of scale. If you identified through your analysis that no company has established a leadership position in a particular market, there may be an opportunity for your company to become leader.

One tool that is helpful in clarifying your marketing strategy is a SWOT framework. Here are a few questions to consider in assessing your strengths, weaknesses, opportunities, and threats:

1. Capitalize on Strengths

• Where are you successful? Why? How can this area grow?

• Are there elements of your offering that clients particularly value that you could better promote?

• Have you created a new process or product that perfectly meets customer needs?

2. Diminish Weaknesses

• Where are you losing share or money? Why?

• Are your competitors taking share—which segment are they focusing on and with what value proposition?

• Can this area be improved or should it be eliminated?

• Are there knowledge and/or capability gaps?

3. Pursue Opportunities

• Are customers demanding solutions that fit your company's existing capabilities or capabilities you could develop?

• Where are your competitors losing? Why? Can you pick up their dissatisfied customers by promoting a particular service or benefit?

• Are there emerging markets that are lucrative for you to pursue?

4. Mitigate Threats

• Where are competitors heading? Do you have the resources to compete with them? Do you want to?

• Are there changes in market demand? Any new entrants? Are there new regulations that will affect the industry?

Now you're ready to define the marketing strategy. As I mentioned previously, I don't think the four Ps are relevant to most companies at this stage. What's more relevant are these three areas:

1. Target Market(s): Who are the target markets (usually segments within the overall market) that you're going to pursue? Which segment(s) best fit your company's capabilities, strengths, and goals? Which segment will you pursue first, and then next? You can't pursue them all; this activity is all about prioritizing.

2. Value Proposition: Why should people buy from you instead of your competitors? What are your specific, objective, and quantified competitive advantages for each of your target markets (they usually differ between segments). Be very clear here—don't fall back on business jargon or vague statements.

3. Messaging: What words will you use to spark interest among your target market? Your messaging will be based on your value proposition. The focus should be on pain points—your messaging needs to address your target market's pains.

These exercises are the practical approach to developing an effective marketing strategy. You should be able to present your strategy in ten to fifteen PowerPoint slides—

or six to nine pages of text. If it's longer, you need to continue refining it

Your strategy is the foundation for all your marketing activities.

CHAPTER 8: MOVING FROM STRATEGY TO REALITY

What's a tactical B2B marketing plan

Without a strategy, marketing tactics are often just a haphazard collection of ideas. But B2B marketing effectiveness lies in translating that strategy into action through tactical planning.

A tactical B2B marketing plan outlines:

• What will be executed—A clear list of the marketing tactics that will be undertaken based on the marketing goals.

• When tactics will happen—A calendar that outlines the timing of tactics and activities.

• Who will be responsible for implementing—A detailed schedule of the amount of time and other resources required along with responsibilities for who has input and who is in charge.

• How much money will be spent—The budget for each tactic.

• Why the tactic is being undertaken—How performance will be measured, primarily the outcomes and metrics the team will use to gauge success.

In this section, I describe how to create the components of the tactical plan—how to choose tactics, create a realistic timeline, and determine the resources required.

How do you choose the right tactics for your company?

One of the most common challenges for B2B companies is knowing which marketing tactics they should implement. They might hear about a particular tactic, jump on the bandwagon, and then when it doesn't work out, they proclaim, "Marketing doesn't work for our company". Or they might stick with a tactic, because it's common in their industry, or it's the way things have always been done. These techniques lead to ineffective marketing, because a good strategy is all about choosing the right tactics at the right time.

Almost every B2B company wants a standard prescription for marketing tactics. I wish there was such an easy answer. But many factors influence which marketing tactics a company should use:

- The industry

- The target market

- The company's position in the market

- How much marketing the company has done in the past and how successful it has been

- What kind of marketing the competition does

- The company's goals

- The company's marketing budget

I have four guidelines to help companies choose the right tactics.

Guideline 1: Get the basics in place

In my experience, B2B companies focus mainly on sales and product development when starting out. Marketing isn't a major consideration, but some marketing basics are needed to legitimize the company and support the sales team in securing early stage customers. The marketing basics vary by industry but usually include a website (that accurately reflects the company's solutions and value), a company overview, and product technical specification sheets. Other tools that can be helpful include product demonstration videos, ROI calculators, case studies, and testimonials.

For any B2B company, no matter how small, these are the essentials.

Guideline 2: What's your stage of evolution?

Different B2B marketing tactics have impact at different stages of growth—some deliver incredible ROI at one stage and none (or negative) at another.

Phase 1—Education and Awareness

The early stages of most B2B marketing are typically focused on getting pilot clients. The target market doesn't know the company—and in many cases doesn't even know that their solution exists—so it's the role of sales and marketing to educate the market and raise awareness. In Phase 1, marketing investments should educate the market and generate awareness, such as video demonstrations, white papers, telemarketing, and speaking engagements. In some industries, social media works well at this stage. Unless a B2B company is venture-funded and has very aggressive growth goals, the marketing investments should be narrowly focused at this stage. Marketing's primary role is to support the company in securing enough pilot clients to create a track record.

Phase 2—Lead Generation

Once a B2B company has a track record and a story to tell, it can move into a more aggressive expansion period where marketing is looked to for higher ROI. There is no hard line indicating when a company has arrived at this stage, generally an organization will have a sense of confidence that they have enough proof of concept and reference clients to assert themselves in the market. At this stage, B2B companies should add marketing activities that focus on generating leads and leveraging the awareness that was built during Phase One. Examples include SEO, lead nurturing systems, and webinars. To

support these activities, more time must be spent on content development to provide the inputs for the marketing activities.

Developing the tactical plan helps prioritize the marketing tools and initiatives that will fulfill your objectives.

A solid tactical plan is essential for managing the marketing function—without one, it's difficult to monitor performance and determine whether you're making progress.

Phase 3—Brand Building

Just like with one and two, there is no hard and fast line between Phase 2 and Phase 3. A B2B company in Phase 3 has reached a point where it seeks to dominate its industry. Marketing becomes a major investment in order for the company to solidify its brand position. The tactics that it will undertake may be more complex and long-term oriented, such as sponsorships. There is powerful value in being a Phase 3 B2B company—these organizations move to value selling and garner premiums for their expertise and brand rather than purely the widget they produce. The expectation should be that the company gets sole-sourced and is able to secure price premiums over the competition.

Guideline 3—Prioritize Tactics by ROI

Marketing tactics should be chosen based on the results they can deliver, starting with the highest potential ROI to the lowest. The highest value revenues usually come from selling existing products or services to existing customers and the lowest from selling new products or services to new customers

So, what can you do to promote existing products to existing customers? Email is a good choice for staying in touch with customers, keeping them abreast of technical improvements, telling them about new applications for your solutions, and generally reminding them that you exist.

After that, the highest value comes from selling new products to existing customers. Your existing base should be the target for product launches. Invite them to upcoming lunch and learns or webinars to showcase your latest innovations.

Then you can focus on promoting existing products to new customers. Here is where you'll consider tactics like SEO.

And finally, pursue new revenues among new customers. This can be done through, for example, trade shows.

What's interesting is that most companies put this last category first when they think about marketing. But this isn't the place to start, when maximizing ROI is your goal.

Admittedly, this framework isn't entirely black and white. Many tactics cross between quadrants. A trade show might touch all four tactics. All the same, it's a good guideline for evaluating the right tactics for your B2B company.

Guideline 4: Focus Your Efforts and Evolve

The final consideration when choosing tactics is this: don't try to do too much at once. If you try to do too much, you'll end up doing a poor job of everything. You're better off beginning with a handful of tactics that are clearly aligned with your goals, and focusing your effort on executing those tactics well. If you're just starting out in marketing, pick three to five tactics over your first six months. More sophisticated companies, or those who are leveraging outside support and expertise, can work with five to twelve. If you do a good job implementing your priority tactics, you'll get results—and that will enable you to evolve your marketing program with confidence—and higher profits.

Integrating tactics to nurture B2B relationships

There is no silver bullet in B2B marketing. While individual tactics are effective methods of increasing exposure and driving leads, no tactic alone is as effective as multiple tactics used together. All B2B marketing tactics are more effective when used as part of an integrated marketing plan. B2C companies create television, radio, digital, and print marketing efforts to make sure consumers hear their message frequently and repeatedly; similarly, B2B companies need to integrate their tactics to build awareness of their solutions.

For example, a telemarketing campaign might work for your business, but it will be much more effective if combined with an email that informs the recipient that you'll be calling, an invitation to an upcoming webinar, and then a follow-up invitation to an event at a local, industry trade show. The golden rule is that it takes five to seven touches before your name will register on the typical, busy person's radar. So integrating tactics is essential to get B2B buyers to hear and understand your message.

The other reason to integrate tactics is that it enables your company to nurture relationships. The B2B purchase cycle is long, so it's unlikely to land on a potential buyer's radar and have them buy the next week. B2B relationships must be nurtured over time, providing the right type and amount of information and expertise to move prospects one step further in the sales process. Integrating tactics enables you to do this—you can provide a white paper, a webinar, an email newsletter with recent case studies, and an invitation to a local lunch and learn over the course of weeks or months. This allows you to build relationships with prospects. The growing number of lead-nurturing systems makes it much more cost effective than in the pasT.

How do you create a realistic action plan?

Putting together a marketing calendar requires realistic thinking about what tactics you can undertake with your resources. If you're using an outside firm or firms to support your marketing, you have an advantage in that they will carry the bulk of the workload. But don't assume that your time won't be needed—it will. No outside firm can undertake B2B marketing in a vacuum. If they try, they won't be able to create as valuable of a product—they simply won't have enough of your technical knowledge to develop and distribute the content that is needed to establish you as a leader.

I suggest two ways for developing a realistic marketing calendar. The first is the "work-back" plan:

a) Determine your total capacity. For example, if you have a part-time marketing resource (half of an FTE), your marketing capacity is roughly eighty hours per month.

b) Identify your fixed marketing activities—the major industry conferences, trade shows, and other events. Enter these on your marketing calendar along with relevant deadlines, such as the deadline for shipping the booth.

c) Identify the tactics related to those fixed events and estimate the time needed for them.

- If you're using your own resources for marketing, especially if you're starting marketing with minimal infrastructure in place, be prepared for tasks to take longer than predicted. To be safe, add 10-20% to the amount of time you've initially estimated.

- Think about the inputs to the fixed events—for example, are you rebranding and need to incorporate the new corporate identity into the trade show materials? These need precede the other activities, so make sure to add them to your critical path.

d) Earmark 10% of your total capacity to allow for marketing opportunities that arise—they always do. Leave more if your company is growing rapidly.

e) Calculate your remaining capacity by subtracting the time required for fixed activities (step c) and for unallocated activities (step d) from your total capacity (step a).

f) Identify your remaining marketing tactics and the amount of time needed to execute them. Enter them on the calendar until you've run out of capacity.

This approach helps companies be realistic about marketing resources and what can be accomplished. The drawback is that it's possible to allocate time and resources to the wrong tactics—for example, what if the fixed events shouldn't, in fact, be the highest priority tactics?

The second approach is the "work-up" plan:

a) Identify the marketing that you want to do from highest priority to lowest.

b) Estimate the amount of time required for individual tactics.

c) Enter tactics and hours on the calendar, respecting the fixed events (time-specific, third-party events) and building tactics around them as appropriate.

d) Spread out your marketing initiatives over the year to balance out capacity as much as possible, recognizing that some activities simply have to be done at certain times.

e) Evaluate what amount of resources you need—is it a part-time resource, full-time resource, a number of vendors?

This approach helps identify what resources are needed to execute your marketing tactics. The drawback—very few companies have the resources to do everything they want to do.

I find a combination of these two approaches is the best way to get a realistic calendar that prioritizes the right tactics.

Most companies need three to six months of operating with their marketing calendar to have a strong sense of what they can really accomplish. The efficiency and project management skills of your marketing resources will determine how much can be accomplished.

What should your B2B marketing budget be?

So how much should you spend on marketing? There is surprisingly little standard information on this topic. It's one of the most common questions I hear from CEOs—they simply don't know what's reasonable.

Every company has a different approach to marketing and needs different tactics, therefore a different marketing budget is needed for every company. Factors that affect a company's marketing budget include the nature of its industry, its business goals (especially related to growth targets), the size and stage or evolution of the company, its target market, the position it wants to take in the industry, and its distribution model.

With those caveats, here are some guidelines. The 2012 Marketing Sherpa study of 1,745 B2B marketers provides the following benchmarks:

- 48% of B2B companies spend 1-5% of gross revenue on marketing

- 25% of companies spend 6-10% of gross revenue on marketing

- The remaining 27% of B2B companies spend more than 10%

This is a good guideline for companies that are newer to the marketing function. If you are just starting out, allocate in the 1-5% range, and as you build competence, you'll have every reason to expand. Companies that are more sophisticated, and understand how to get ROI from marketing, tend to increase their spend from year to year—which makes sense, because as they make more money through marketing, they want to do more of it.

Many companies wonder about the breakdown between marketing staff and marketing programs (e.g., trade shows, print advertising, pay-per-click, SEO). This metric used to be a good gauge of the efficiency of a marketing team. Companies would aim to get their staff costs down to a percentage of total budget. Smaller companies tended to have staff costs around 50%, and larger companies (with larger spend and therefore efficiency) would spend closer to 20%.

The 2012 Marketing Sherpa study indicated that 70% of the 1,745 B2B company participants spent between 5% and 30% of their budget on in-house staff. The remaining 30% of firms spent 30% to 90%.

This data demonstrates a shift in marketing behaviour. B2B tactics that involve labour (e.g., content development and social media) are on the rise, while tactics that involve tangible goods (e.g., brochures and pens) are in decline. I expect this shift will continue, and there will be fewer questions around the breakdown of budgets and more questions on overall ROI. At the end of the day, it's all about how much profitable revenue the marketing program generates.

Who should do the marketing?

Small and mid-size B2B companies face a challenge in finding the right level and amount of resources to effectively manage marketing.

There are several options for B2B companies to get the right resource mix for effective marketing.

In-house Senior Marketer (VP, CMO)

Having an in-house senior marketing executive is an aspiration for many B2B companies. An executive responsible for marketing allows the company to have marketing expertise (assuming the right person was hired) to make good, strategic decisions about marketing investments. It means that someone at the leadership level is bringing marketing issues to the fore, and these issues are being considered when making investments in other departments (e.g., the marketing impact of customer service decisions).

However, the majority of small and mid-size B2B companies don't need, and can't afford, a senior marketing executive. Their salary isn't justified based on the marketing spend and needs of the company. So, while having a marketing executive is appealing for small and mid-size B2B companies, for most it's not practical. Companies that have over fifty million in revenue and spend more than one million annually in marketing usually need senior marketing leadership. Below this level, it depends on the company's strategy and industry.

In-house Junior Marketer (Coordinator, Manager)

When most B2B companies begin to get serious about marketing, they start out by hiring someone at a junior level. A full-time junior marketer can do a lot—and there is usually a lot to be done.

But the downside to junior marketing personnel is that they often don't have strategic marketing skills. They don't know which marketing tactics make sense given the company's overall business strategy. They must be managed and directed by a manager in the company, which can be challenging if that manager has a busy schedule. Junior marketing personnel are also more likely to leave the company. If they are focused on developing their careers, they will crave opportunities to take on new challenges, which they may achieve by jumping from one company to the next. This is difficult because it creates gaps between marketers, which brings inconsistency in execution. Management will need to dedicate time to identifying and then orienting new personnel.

And, of course, there's the challenge of finding good junior talent—people with a great work ethic and the ability to fit into the culture of a particular organization.

Senior / Junior Mix

Having a combination of senior and junior marketers is a good way to achieve strategic marketing that is consistently executed. The senior marketer should be responsible for setting the strategy, determining tactics, investment levels and the scorecard, and advocating for marketing within the company's leadership team. The senior person should also handle some of the execution activities, such as setting up strategic alliances and the thought leadership program. The junior marketer will be responsible primarily for execution and should be overseen by the senior.

The drawback to this approach is that many B2B companies simply don't need two full-time marketing resources given the limited size of their marketing program.

Part-Time Senior Independent Contractor

One way for a B2B company that doesn't have an extensive marketing program to achieve the level of strategy needed is to contract a senior independent marketer. If the company can find a marketing executive who has relevant experience, and retain them on an ongoing, part-time basis, they can access the expertise they need. To make this work, a coordinator or manager will also be needed to handle execution, as the senior person will not be cost effective (and likely not interested) in this component of the marketing function.

There are two potential drawbacks to this approach. The first is sustainability. If the independent contractor is between jobs and takes a full-time role with another company, you may be left without a resource and have to start the process of finding a marketer all over again. The second is a question of skill. Does the independent have experience and knowledge in the tactics that make sense for your company? If not, they are likely to adopt the tactics they have experience in—and these might end up wasting your investment rather than growing your business. Be sure to vet any independents before retaining them to ensure they have the skills and experience to direct your marketing appropriately.

Hybrid Solution (outsourced marketing management)

There are B2B marketing outsourcing firms that provide a strategic marketing plan developed by a team of experts, and then the resources to execute the plan on an ongoing basis. My company, The Mezzanine Group, provides this kind of service.

This model is fairly new and different companies have different approaches. Some work on-site at the client's location, others work off-site. Some handle everything under a full-service model, others do certain pieces but will also use clients' admin or junior staff.

This approach gives B2B companies access to marketing strategy expertise and then resources to execute cost efficiently. They can provide better marketing results, because they know what tactics to use and how to implement them. They're more accountable than in-house staff because of the nature of their contracts with clients, and they enable the company's management team to devote less time to managing marketing than would be possible with an in-house solution.

The downside is that they cost more than an in-house marketing resource on an hour-for-hour basis.

Systems to make marketing efficient

Like every business function, marketing performs best when it is actively managed. Most B2B companies don't do a good job of consistently managing their marketing. They find they don't have time, and then wonder why their marketing isn't performing well. If you're taking the time to read this book, I assume you're interested in achieving effective marketing. Proper management is the place to start.

The building blocks of effective marketing management are:

a) Have a marketing plan to guide activities and clarify goals

b) Dedicate an appropriate level and quantity of resources (time, money)

c) Meet weekly to review and discuss progress with the people who are executing

d) Recalibrate the plan as needed to respond to opportunities and challenges

e) Report activities and results on a monthly basis.

Easy, right? Somehow it's tougher in reality, but having the right senior resources will address the common challenges in marketing management. One of the best methods, once you have a marketing plan and someone responsible for executing it, is holding weekly meetings (building block c). Doing this will make it clear—quickly—if you have the right resources for your marketing and whether or not your plan is doable.

Be flexible in your approach if you're new to marketing. Market conditions can change, new forces can affect buyer behaviour, and other, unforeseen circumstances can affect your marketing program. Be prepared to reassess, recalibrate, and adjust timing of marketing tactics as you proceed with implementation and are regularly measuring performance. Below are a few tips and questions to ask over the course of the year to ensure that your marketing is adapting to changes in conditions.

- Is your marketing achieving the goals you set

- Which tools and tactics are working and which aren't?

- Are some tactics delivering better results than others? If so, can you move budget and activity into those areas and away from others?

Timing

In the majority of B2B environments where the sales cycle is long and complex, it takes time for marketing to make an impact.

- It will take 1-8 weeks to see marketing activity (e.g. press releases, website updates)
- It will take 4-12 weeks to see marketing results (better search engine rankings, media mentions of stories in industry publications)
- It will take 6-24 weeks to see an increase in the number of leads
- It will take 8-52 weeks to see new deals as a result of marketing (typically, the bigger the deals, the longer it takes)

If your initial results aren't hitting your targets, it doesn't necessarily mean you're on the wrong track. It does take time, and finding the right mix of marketing tactics is a balance that few companies get perfect the first time around. After two to three months, sit down and evaluate what you've been doing, how well you've been executing, and what the results are. If things are going in the right direction but aren't delivering the quantity of results you're looking for, you may need to devote more time to marketing.

If you feel you aren't executing well, take a look at your resources and plan—are you trying to do too much with too little? If you aren't getting any good results and things don't seem to be going in the right direction, look at the deeper issues—is your strategy (business or marketing) sound, are you using the right tactics, is your message on the mark? Then recalibrate your plan and keep going.

How to set goals for B2B marketing

There are two things to measure in B2B marketing—activities and results. Some companies argue that all that matters is results, and indeed, that's ultimately true, but it's easier to evaluate the results when you know the level of activity being applied.

It's important to balance the measurement of both activities and results. I've seen many companies get distracted by the amount of marketing activity and forget about getting results. I've also seen companies expect significant results and then not execute the activities. Both matter.

It would be nice if there was a standard prescription for setting marketing goals. Unfortunately, there isn't. However, in the sections on tactics, I provide a number of metrics that address both the activity and result considerations.

You can compile the individual tactic metrics into a marketing scorecard that includes five to ten metrics that you will track and report on monthly. Some metrics may be leading indicators (for example, leads will help predict revenues) and others will be lagging. The purpose is to focus your marketing team on the activities that matter most to your business success and for everyone to get a view into what results are being achieved.

CHAPTER 9: DEVELOPING CONTENT

Why do you need content?

One of the biggest differences between B2B and consumer marketing is thought leadership. A thought leader is a company or individual recognized for their expertise in a particular area. A thought leader can guide their industry towards the implementation and application of new ideas. Being recognized as a thought leader makes you the "go-to" for particular products or services and is a powerful way to increase brand equity, achieve price premiums, and avoid bid competition.

B2B companies need to be thought leaders in order to dominate their industries. But how do you become recognized as a thought leader?

The starting point is to have deep expertise in a particular area and a demonstrated track record. If you don't have proof that your solution works, your first step is to get that proof. Without it, buyers won't have any evidence of your expertise or qualifications—making it less likely that they'll choose to buy from you. This means that any marketing you do without a track record might be dollars badly spent.

Once you have a track record, the next step is to establish your reputation as a thought leader. This happens by sharing your experience and expertise through content, such as white papers, case studies, blogs, and articles.

Generating content is simple to plan but much harder to execute. I've seen many companies recognize the importance of generating content, commit to it wholeheartedly, and then fall on their faces within three months. I'll even admit that one of those companies was Mezzanine in its early years.

The good news: it gets easier with experience, but it takes continued commitment and resources, and some systems and processes.

There are two parts to content development—deciding what content to produce and producing it.

How do you decide what topics to cover?

Some companies struggle with what kind of content to produce—they don't realize they have expertise that can be turned into compelling material. Here are some practical ways to identify and qualify content ideas:

1. Generate a list of twenty topics and ask your customer-facing staff (business development, customer service) to rate the topics. Since these employees talk with customers every day, they understand what's important to them. They know what questions they get asked, and they know what is currently selling.

2. Repeat the process of gathering topics, but have a customer advisory panel rate the topics. A customer advisory panel usually consists of five to ten customers that have a good relationship with your company and that represent your full customer base. Send each customer a personalized email and have them rate each topic. Most importantly, make it dead easy for them. The process should only take five minutes of their time; you're looking for a gut reaction to the topics.

3. Take your product developers (often engineers) to lunch, talk to them, and take notes. During these lunch meetings, get the engineers to talk about your products or services; their passion and enthusiasm for the product will

come across naturally. If you are in a highly technical industry, get them to explain the most technical aspects of the product and why they're useful to customers. After you've spoken to several different engineers, gather up your notes and create content ideas.

As a final step, cross-reference your topic list against upcoming product launches, your firm's core competencies, market trends, and changing customer needs to ensure the topics are well-aligned with your strategy.

Through this process, create an editorial calendar for the year. What topics will you cover and when? Should some topics come before others? Are some topics relevant at particular times of the year or business cycle?

How do you produce content?

The reality of B2B marketing is that content needs to come, in good measure, from the thought leaders. Unfortunately, they don't always enjoy the process of disseminating their expertise. Ask an engineer to write a white paper, and he or she will be happy to do it—but you'll be lucky to see it within a few months.

The best way to produce content for B2B marketing is to make it very easy for the technical experts to contribute—which means not forcing them to produce content all alone.

 A good approach is to choose a topic and interview a technical expert for thirty to sixty minutes, capturing as much knowledge as possible, and then prepare a first draft of the piece. It won't be perfect, but it will be something the expert can respond to. Book more time with him or her and get verbal feedback. Thendo another draft and work this way, on a timeline, until completion.

Another approach is to hire a third party to develop the content. The pressure of having someone else involved can be a good motivator to keep the technical experts moving.

Sales Support Collateral

Every B2B company needs basic collateral that supports the sales team when presenting to potential customers. However, the nature of those materials has changed over the last decade. The extensive, glossy brochures of the past are no longer the norm, and it's more likely that the sales team will need digital versions of their materials to send prospects before and after sales meetings.

One of the most common sales support documents is a professionally prepared overview of the company with information on its history, management team, expertise, and solution set (products, services, or combination).

Technical specification sheets are still common in engineered solutions, although they don't need to be pre-printed. More companies are using digital printing to produce materials as needed rather than printing thousands of copies through a traditional printing process. Formatted correctly, spec sheets are easy to make accessible on your website, which makes it simple and fast for your sales team, agents, and prospects to obtain them.

Other sales support collateral options are case studies and white papers.

And lastly, don't forget business cards. Some argue they're on the decline with more people exchanging contact information electronically. That's true in some industries, but the majority of B2B companies still operate in the tangible world. Focus on high quality when purchasing business cards. It's easy to get inexpensive ones, so lots of people do. But there is a difference between high-quality business cards and the overused, standard, stock ones. It's a small thing that can make a big difference at the first impression stage.

Case Studies

Case studies are a high-impact tool that allows B2B companies to demonstrate their experience and track record. A customer speaking positively on your behalf is one of the greatest sources of credibility for your company, and the ability to tell a story about actual results is much stronger than any elevator pitch.

Case studies can serve as a useful sales support tool as content on your website, as input to articles, and as the basis for speaking engagements. They can also be used as part of your lead nurturing process.

It's important to have multiple case studies. Having only one may seem questionable to potential buyers (Does that mean you only have one client? Or only one who would speak on your behalf? Have you had favourable results only once?) A single case study may be worse for your image than none. I recommend a minimum of three but five to eight is ideal. If you serve multiple industries and situations, separate the case studies into categories, so readers can easily find the case studies most relevant to them.

If you're in the enviable position of having numerous experiences that could turn into case studies, make the choice based on these factors:

a) The biggest / most impressive customer names (sanitized case studies—i.e. those where the customer can't be named—are less effective).

b) The best business results—focus on the quantifiable results of dollars ($), percentages (%), and numbers (#). Anything with those symbols catch readers' eyes and speak directly to their needs.

c) The most relevant to your marketing goals, so that your most coveted prospects will find something that will help you sell to them.

When developing a portfolio of case studies, create examples that cover the range of benefits you deliver and the range of industries you serve. Start by drawing a matrix of the industries, benefits, and results you want to showcase, and then identify potential case studies that fit into each of those categories.

How To Develop A Case Study

When embarking on your first case study, it's important to develop a framework to serve as a template for future case studies. This will save you time down the road.

Case studies typically follow a basic framework of challenge- solution-results. A successful case study layout covers eight key components:

1. A profile of the customer

2. An explanation of the challenge

3. An explanation of how your company's product/service fixed their problem

4. Clear summary of the results/ROI

5. Testimonials or quotes

6. Bold title

7. Strong visuals

8. A brief "About Us" (typically on the last page of your case study) with a link to your website where prospects can learn more.

Case studies should be one to two pages; four is acceptable if you have a lot to say and need more space for visuals and technical drawings. Any longer—unless the product / solution is particularly complex—and you will lose your audience.

It's tempting when you're writing case studies to go with the easiest customer first—the one you have the best relationship with, and the one you know will be happy to sign off on anything you develop. That's a fine way to get going. But be mindful that it isn't where you stop. Think strategically about your target market, and which customer situation is most like the customers you want to attract. It's ok to start with the easy ones, but make sure to keep going and tackle the harder—and more valuable—case study options.

In order to gather the information you need for your case study, you'll likely need to interview your client. Keep your interviews simple and structured. Send them the questions in advance, so they know what you want to cover. Here's a structure I use as a starting point (always adapt it to the specific client and situation):

Challenge

- Describe the business problem/challenge that needed to be solved.

- Have you tried to solve this problem in the past?

- What impact did this problem have on your business?

Solution

- How did you hear about our company?
- How did you decide to use our company for your solution?
- Describe the solution and how it was implemented.
- Comment on the people you worked with at our company.
- How long did it take to implement?

Results

- How did the solution help solve the problem/challenge?
- What benefits did you derive from the solution?

- What has been the measurable impact on your business from deploying this solution? (Focus on quantifiable results—$, %, #.)
- Have there been any "soft" benefits from the solution?

Make sure to capture the customer's verbatim comments during the interview so they can be turned into quotes and testimonials in the case study (and elsewhere). Once you've completed a draft, have the customer review and sign off on it.

If your client is unable to provide authorization to use their name, you can do a case that describes their industry, geography, and position in the market. It's not as credible without the client name, but it's better than no case study at all. Sometimes it is difficult or impossible for clients to sign off on case studies; larger corporations have policies that often constrain this.

Once you have a portfolio of case studies, begin integrating them into your marketing program. Feature them on your website, turn them into industry presentations or webinars, do PR around them, and use them throughout the business development process.

www.ingramcontent.com/pod-product-compliance
Lightning Source LLC
Chambersburg PA
CBHW052323220526

45472CB00001B/246